FEARNOT!

MEDITATIONS TO OVERCOME FEAR, WORRY, AND DISCOURAGEMENT

RAND HUMMEL

JOURNEYFORTH

Greenville, South Carolina

Library of Congress Cataloging-in-Publication Data

Hummel, Rand, 1956-
    Fear not! : meditations to overcome fear, worry, and discouragement / Rand Hummel.
        p. cm.
    Summary: "This is a book of meditations to overcome fear, worry, and discouragement"—Provided by publisher.
    ISBN 978-1-59166-870-1 (perfect bound pbk. : alk. paper)
    1. Anxiety—Religious aspects—Christianity—Meditations. 2. Fear—Religious aspects—Christianity—Meditations. 3. Worry—Religious aspects—Christianity—Meditations. 4. Depression, Mental—Religious aspects—Christianity—Meditations. I. Title.
    BV4908.5.H86 2008
    242'.4--dc22
                                                            2008007638

Photo Credits: iStockPhoto.com (cover and sand)
I'm Adopted by Ron Hamilton © 1987 by Majesty Music, Inc. All rights reserved.

All Scripture is quoted from the Authorized King James Version.

Fear Not! Meditations to Overcome Fear, Worry, and Discouragement

Design by Elly Kalagayan
Page layout by Kelley Moore

© 2008 by BJU Press
Greenville, South Carolina 29614
JourneyForth is a division of BJU Press

Printed in the United States of America

ISBN 978-1-59166-870-1

15   14   13   12   11   10   9   8   7   6   5   4   3   2   1

CONTENTS

■ ■ ■

Part Two: God's Word applied to ten common fears

FEAR NOT . . .
FOR THE LORD WILL
DO GREAT THINGS.

Joel 2:21

INTRODUCTION

■ ■ ■

Dear Reader,

What do you fear? What worries you? Has discouragement stolen your joy? Fear, anxiety, worry, lack of trust, discouragement, and hopelessness are a part of life today. Combine high-stress lifestyles, uncontrolled difficulties, and hopeless situations, and we can see why fear and worry have such a stranglehold on our society. Life is not fair, but God's love never changes. Life is not easy, but God's grace is always sufficient. Life is confusing, but God's purpose is always Christlikeness. Life's challenges are at times insurmountable, but God's power is always available.

There is good fear and bad fear. The fear that would cause us to run from a fire, flee from a wild animal, or teach our children to stay out of the street when they play is a good fear. It is necessary for preservation. The fear that comes from sudden alarm can help us to make quick decisions that could save lives. The fear or dread of standing face to face with a holy God is a good fear that results in wisdom, knowledge, contentment, fleeing from evil, confidence, and satisfaction. (The book of Proverbs is full of such promises to those who fear God.) The bad kind of fear finds its roots in faithlessness and can torment us or enslave us to irrational and unspiritual decisions. The fear of the future keeps us from trusting in a sovereign God. The fear of man can suffocate the life right out of us as we are prone to give in to the fear embarrassment, rejection, bodily harm, or even death. Worry, anxiety, discouragement, and the wrong kind of fear can be defined simply as a lack of trust in a trustworthy God.

The simple meditations found in this book are designed to challenge us to meditate on the very words of God in such a way that the deceitfulness and wickedness of our sin are clearly exposed and that our hope for victory over debilitating fear is finally realized. How can we change the way we handle fear, worry, and discouragement? By guarding our hearts and minds with the very words of God. Please do not get in a hurry. Take your time, even if it means taking three years to get through this book. Think. Meditate. Spend time with each word and word meaning until the truth of what God is saying becomes a part of your life.

Remember, there is no excuse and we don't have to worry. "There hath no temptation taken you but such as is common to man: but God is faithful, who will not suffer you to be tempted above that ye are able; but will with the temptation also make a way to escape, that ye may be able to bear it" (1 Corinthians 10:13). Meditating on the truths of God's Word discussed in this book hopefully will be your way of escape.

Fear Not!
Rand Hummel

MEDITATION

■ ■ ■

LET'S THINK ABOUT IT.

Meditation is essential for anyone who desires to handle fear, worry, and discouragement God's way. Much of the information in this chapter was covered in the first book of this series, *Lest You Fall*. The same principles of meditation apply whether you are wrestling with impurity, anger, bitterness, fear, or worry.

The word translated "meditation" throughout Scripture is also translated "imagine" (Ps. 2:1; 38:12), "studieth" (Prov. 15:28; 24:2), "utter, mutter, talk, or speak" (Job 27:4; Ps. 37:30; 71:24; Prov. 8:7), and "mourn" (Isa. 16:7; 38:14; 59:11). It is usually defined as "murmuring," or speaking to oneself. How often do we as believers devote a full morning to studying, imagining, talking through, or speaking to ourselves (meditating) about one specific characteristic of God taught in His Word?

Meditation is a form of creative thinking. Through word studies, comparisons with other passages, and a good study Bible we can understand what God is saying and how to apply it in a life-changing way. For instance, if we set aside an entire hour to "think about" or meditate on how much God loves righteousness and hates evil, our thinking will be affected in such a way that we will personally begin loving good and hating evil more.

Meditation is essential for a full understanding of God's Word. Most of us have developed lazy habits in reading, grammar, syntax, and word study. We often glance over a word we think we know rather than gaze into its true intent and purpose. When Paul uses the phrase "for this cause" (Rom. 1:26; Eph. 5:31; 2 Thess. 2:11, and so forth), it is so easy to just keep reading rather than to stop and think, "What cause?" "What is this driving force in Paul's life?" "What was his essential reason for living?" "What is my ultimate reason, purpose, or cause for living?" "Have I attached myself to a cause bigger than myself, my wants, my time, and my life?" Now Paul's simple phrase "for this cause" takes on a new relevance and my heart is convicted because I have been living for my own "causes" and not God's!

Meditation is essential for all who seek victory over fear, worry, and discouragement. Failure in paralyzing fear, debilitating worry, or hopeless discouragement comes from a lack of knowledge, a misunderstanding of Bible principles, or a misapplication of scriptural truths. We may have read many of the passages that deal with the sin of fear and worry but have not thought about them in a way that impacts our hearts. The purpose of this book is to encourage those who desire to free themselves from the bondage of fear and worry to meditate on the very words of God that deal with such temptations. What God has already given us in His written Word are the very words He would speak to us if we were in a one-on-one counseling situation with Him. As you will see, we will meditate on over 140 verses from 40-plus passages that specifically deal with fear, worry, and discouragement. At the end of this book, you can take what you have learned and meditate on other passages of Scripture that deal with all kinds of life issues in the same way.

We can live joyful, secure, confident lives free from bondage to the sins of fear and worry as we begin thinking like God thinks. That takes time! That takes energy! That takes meditation! Now, let's think about it.

"Meditate upon these things; give thyself wholly to them; that thy profiting may appear to all." *(1 Tim. 4:15)*

Meditation should delight us!

"I will meditate in thy precepts, and have respect unto thy ways. I will delight myself in thy statutes: I will not forget thy word." *(Ps. 119:15–16)*

"Blessed is the man that walketh not in the counsel of the ungodly, nor standeth in the way of sinners, nor sitteth in the seat of the scornful. But his delight is in the law of the Lord; and in his law doth he meditate day and night." *(Ps. 1:1–2)*

"My meditation of him shall be sweet: I will be glad in the Lord." *(Ps. 104:34)*

Meditation should consume us!

"Let the words of my mouth, and the meditation of my heart, be acceptable in thy sight, O Lord, my strength, and my redeemer." *(Ps. 19:14)*

"O how love I thy law! It is my meditation all the day." *(Ps. 119:97)*

"Mine eyes prevent the night watches, that I might meditate in thy word." *(Ps. 119:148)*

Meditation should control us!

"This book of the law shall not depart out of thy mouth; but thou shalt meditate therein day and night, that thou mayest observe to do according to all that is written therein: for then thou shalt make thy way prosperous, and then thou shalt have good success." *(Josh. 1:8)*

The Mechanics of MEDITATION

■ ■ ■

"How Do You Do This?"

In some areas of life, there is danger in being a "do-it-yourselfer." I know enough about working on cars to get a job started but often not enough to finish it. Some "do-it-yourself" plumbers, with the goal of simply replacing a faucet, can turn their bathroom into a water park complete with fountains and pools. There are other times when it is essential to be a "do-it-yourselfer." Meditation is one of those times. It is something that we must learn to do ourselves. We can read books, listen to messages, and allow others to meditate for us or we can study, labor, and master the art of meditation for ourselves. This is definitely a do-it-yourself discipline of the Christian life.

Anyone can meditate. Everyone should meditate. Most don't even try. If you were not interested in controlling your fear and learning to meditate on what God has to say about faithless worry, you probably would not even be reading this book. What you need is a meditation toolbox that is filled with the proper meditation tools. I would encourage you to get one tool at a time and practice using it until you have mastered it. Don't fall into the trap of filling up your toolbox with specialty tools that you never use.

Tool 1: Your Bible

Read . . . read . . . READ! Read the passage you are studying over and over again. I sometimes type the book or passage out to myself in letter form without any verse or chapter markings. I start with the letter addressed to myself.

Dear Rand,

Type the passage and then end the letter with the author's name.

Your friend,
Paul, Peter, John or whoever

Tool 2: A study Bible

Study Bibles are a tremendous help in understanding the intent and purpose of any given passage. Sometimes a simple clarification of the audience, customs, geographical considerations, or unusual word usages can help you to understand what God was saying to those people at that time. Bible scholars have given their lives to help those who may not have the time or the training to fully understand why God wrote what He wrote in His Word.

Tool 3: Word-study helps

There are many words in our English Bible whose meanings have changed over the years and have almost become obsolete in conversation today. Words such as *concupiscence, superfluity, wantonness, lasciviousness, lucre, guile,* and *quickened* are not found in most of the letters, e-mails, or text messages we read on a daily basis. Word-study helps such as *Strong's Concordance, Vine's Expository Dictionary, Zodhiates, Robertson's New Testament Word Pictures, Vincent's New Testament Word Studies, Theological Wordbook of the Old Testament,* and

Greek and Hebrew lexicons open up the meanings to words we commonly glance over as we read. Words are powerful. Because we often do not know the true meanings of certain words, we miss their intent and cannot personally apply the passage as we should.

Tool 4: Bible dictionaries and encyclopedias

Most of us have not grown up in the Holy Land, lived in Egypt, or sailed the Mediterranean. I personally have never fished with a net, hunted with a bow, or plowed with an ox. A good Bible dictionary or encyclopedia can help you feel the heat of the desert and understand the difficulty of sailing through a stormy sea. I would suggest *International Standard Bible Encyclopedia* (ISBE), *Zondervan Pictorial Bible Dictionary*, *Nelson's New Illustrated Bible Dictionary*, or *Unger's Bible Dictionary* to start with.

Tool 5: Commitment of time

All the tools available are to no avail without a commitment of time and a commitment to concentration. Meditation takes time. We seem to have the time to do what we want but not the time to do what we should. Consistency in spending extended periods of time in

God's Word is a key to proper meditation. Anytime is a good time, but if you give God, say, one-half hour every morning before you get pulled into your fast and furious daily routine, you will actually wake up in the morning looking forward to spending that time with God. (By the way, if you think you are too busy, consider that this kind of meditation in God's Word will simply replace the wasted time it takes to sin.)

Tool 6: A set place

Finding the right place to ensure complete concentration is also a must. Unless you have a set place to meditate, distractions can easily cause your mind to drift. Find a place where you are isolated, or at least insulated, from the distractions of TV, newspapers, radio, children, friends, and weariness. Find a place where it is just you and God and it is almost like the whole world disappears for those few minutes each morning.

Tool 7: Prayer

Talk to God. Ask God to open your eyes and your heart to what He is saying. Ask God for wisdom; He promises to give it to you. Ask God for understanding;

He wants you to understand. Ask God for insight into His heart. Ask God to help you think as He thinks, to look at sin as He looks at sin, to love kindness and forgiveness as He loves kindness and forgiveness. Your goal is to defeat the fear in your heart by having the mind of Christ. When your meditation becomes your mindset, you will be amazed at your understanding of Scripture and your progress in consistent victory over selfish, sinful thinking. You'll also be pleasing God and not self.

Before we step into the heart of this book, let's walk through one short passage using the tools mentioned above. What is God saying to us in Proverbs 12:25? What words do we need to study and understand so we do not miss their meaning and intent? What word pictures do these words bring to mind that will help us not only fully understand what they are saying but also apply in such a way that they evoke a stronger love for God and a more intense hatred for sin?

This is what God says.

Proverbs 12:25
Heaviness in the heart of man maketh it stoop: but a good word maketh it glad.

Now think about it.

Heaviness (anxiety, fear, and worry) in the heart of man makes it stoop (weighs it down with depression and sadness); but a good word makes it glad, happy, and joyful.

How can this affect me?

When we fill our backpacks with fear, anxiety, and worry, we are so weighted down we can hardly walk. The burden strapped to our back is a constant reminder of our own weakness and our inability to trust God. Our smiles fade as our countenances fall. Our hearts and minds are so consumed with the weight on our backs that we begin the downward spiral of depression that puts more and more anxiety and fear in our backpacks. A "good word" can not only empty the backpack of worry and fear but take the pack off our backs and place it where it belongs in the hands of an almighty God. There are some backpacks too heavy for us, but none too heavy for God. The Bible is a book of God's "good words" that are given to lighten our burdens and trust in Him. When Jesus said, "Take my yoke upon you," He meant it. As we yoke up together with our Lord Jesus Christ, He carries the weight of our heavy burdens. Give your pack to God, sit down, and start digging in His Word to find more of the "good words" that can replace the weightiness of fear, worry, and discouragement with joy, happiness, and gladness.

Part**One**

God's Word Applied to Fear, Worry, and Discouragement

MEDITATION 1

■ ■ ■

FEAR DOES NOT COME FROM GOD.

This is what God says.

2 Timothy 1:7–8

For God hath not given us the spirit of fear; but of power, and of love, and of a sound mind. Be not thou therefore ashamed of the testimony of our Lord, nor of me his prisoner: but be thou partaker of the afflictions of the gospel according to the power of God.

Now think about it.

Our almighty, all-powerful, loving, and caring God has not given us the spirit (the attitude, disposition, or feeling) of fear or dread; but instead He has given us the spirit (the attitude, disposition, or feeling) of power, and the spirit of love, and the spirit of a sound mind. Because of this confident assurance of God's power and love, as you have not been embarrassed or ashamed to be identified with the testimony of our Lord Jesus Christ (and, as far as that goes, even with me as a prisoner, knowing that your association with me could result in your incarceration as well), do not start now to be fearful of the consequences or ashamed of the testimony of our Lord and of me His prisoner: instead be willing to get a taste of the suffering, the ridicule, and the hatred that both the Lord and I have experienced for the sake of the gospel message of redemption. Don't be afraid of such sufferings and afflictions because you will be enabled to deal with them by the glorious power of God.

How can this affect me?

Have you ever thought about the fear that must have gripped Joseph's and Mary's hearts when they heard of Herod's death warrant against their baby Jesus? Their midnight flight to Egypt must have been filled with fright. For a few years they lived as fugitives just because of their identification and connection with Jesus. Do you fear what others may do to you or say about you just because you are a Christian? Do you dread the thought of death, knowing that some hate you and

God so much they may attempt to kill you? Are you scared by the thought of death? Does the thought of persecution of you and your family grip your heart

DREAD DOES NOT COME FROM GOD.

in such a way that you would contemplate turning your back on the God Who loves you? This type of fear and dread does not come from God. If you are facing death (whether it be at the hand of a Christ-hating terrorist or the touch of cancer in your body), God wants to remind you that just as three gifts were placed at the feet of Jesus by the magi to encourage the heart of Mary and Joseph, who were fleeing for their lives, God, the King of Kings, gives you three gifts to drive all dread and fear out of your life.

- The spirit of power: The confidence that you are capable and able to live without fear and dread by the power of an omnipotent, almighty God.

- The spirit of love: The assurance of God's affectionate, purposeful working in our lives, giving us not necessarily what we want but what we need.

- The spirit of a sound mind: The surety of a disciplined mind that thinks clearly and biblically and is not controlled by emotional extremes or lustful tendencies but is controlled by the knowledge that our eternal destiny is in the hands of a powerful and loving God.

This is what God says.

Philippians 4:6–7

Be careful for nothing; but in every thing by prayer and supplication with thanksgiving let your requests be made known unto God. And the peace of God, which passeth all understanding, shall keep your hearts and minds through Christ Jesus.

Now think about it.

Nothing should trouble your heart and fill it with anxiety, fear, or worry. Instead, in the midst of thanking God for everything (everything) in your life, let your requests, your needs, what you lack in life be known to God by prayer (talking directly to Him) and supplication (asking Him to meet your needs). And the peace of God (the tranquility of heart based on the assurance that everything is right between you and God and that He has everything under His sovereign control), which passes all understanding (you just can't explain it but it surpasses and goes far beyond our feeble comprehension), will guard, protect, and keep your heart and mind from worry, fear, and anxiety in Christ Jesus.

How can this affect me?

Let's pretend that it is 1817. Your small cabin is surrounded by a war party with flaming arrows aimed in your direction. Your enemies are closing in from all sides and as a young mother your heart is ready to explode with fear. What will happen to you and your family? If the party captures you, will you be killed right away or slowly tortured? You cry out for your husband, and he and his three brothers come running from the back room with rifles in hand. They take control of the situation as each mans a window on all sides of the cabin. A few shots in the air reveal to the war party that they are not attacking a weak, helpless, and indefensible cabin but a family protected by fighting men who will die to protect this young family. The enemy flees.

Your heart is overcome with fear, worry, apprehension, and anxiety. You feel surrounded and closed in from all sides. There is absolutely no way out of your trouble. What will happen to you and your family? Will you be left all alone? What if someone dies? What if you die? You cry out to God and He reminds you of His promise in Philippians 4:6–7. Talk to God in prayer and watch the fears flee. Trust God through supplications and watch your anxieties dissipate. Thank God for His constant presence, His ever-present protection, and His almighty power. As you talk to God, trust God, and thank God, you will see your enemies turn and run. Your heavenly Father sent His Son not just to protect you from death but to defeat death by rising from the grave. Jesus died to protect you and your family from eternal death. That you can be thankful for! Chase away every fear with thanksgiving. Make worries run with gratitude. Being thankful for what God has done and will do will allow the peace of God to overshadow the fear of heart that we so often struggle with. Surrounded? Fearful? Hopeless? Talk to God, trust God, and thank God. He will protect your heart.

MEDITATION 2

■ ■ ■

NO MATTER HOW SMALL, WEAK, INSIGNIFICANT, OR UNIMPORTANT YOU MAY VIEW YOURSELF, YOU ARE IMPORTANT TO GOD.

This is what God says.

Luke 12:6–7

Are not five sparrows sold for two farthings, and not one of them is forgotten before God? But even the very hairs of your head are all numbered. Fear not therefore: ye are of more value than many sparrows.

Now think about it.

Are not five little sparrows sold for just two pennies? And remember, not one of them is forgotten by God. Why, even the very hairs of your head are all numbered by God. Fear not, don't be afraid; you are worth much more and valued much higher than many sparrows.

How can this affect me?

Can God forget about you? Does God forget about you? Can God forget? How can an all-knowing, omniscient God forget anything? Has He ever forgotten to make the sun rise in the morning or the moon to shine in the evening? Has He ever forgotten to keep the earth spinning on its axis or the ocean to stay within its boundaries? God seeks to comfort our hearts by illustrating His love and concern for us with five sparrows that are worth nothing more than the value of two copper coins (the most worthless of metals compared to silver and gold and the least valuable of all currency of that day). Basically, Jesus was saying that even though those pesky, little birds are not worth two cents to most of us, they are valuable to God (so valuable that He will never forget them). Why? How can these small, chattering, brown and gray birds that swarm over Palestine and feed on seeds, small green buds, tiny insects, and worms have the ever-promised attention of an all-powerful God?

- He created them and will not forget them.

- He gave them the breath of life and will not forget them.
- He designed the shape of their beaks and will not forget them.
- He calculated the strength of their wings and will not forget them.
- He uses them to consume plant-threatening insects and bugs and will not forget them.
- He designed their hunger for seeds to keep the parcel of land from over-seeding and will not forget them.
- He put within them their songs and will not forget them.
- He provides their daily nourishment and will not forget them.
- He chose to remember them and will not forget them.

According to the Lord Himself, you are of more value than many sparrows. If God is so concerned with them, why would you think He would not be concerned with you? Why would you believe that God would forget you? What would make you think that He did not care? Never fear that God will overlook you. Never worry about going through life without anyone caring. God cares. Why?

- He created you and will not forget you.
- He gave you the breath of life and will not forget you.
- He designed your DNA and will not forget you.
- He calculated your gifts and abilities and will not forget you.
- He put within your heart His Holy Spirit and will not forget you.
- He provides your daily needs and will not forget you.
- He has a purpose for your life and will not forget you.
- He chooses to remember you because He loves you and will not forget you.

This is what God says.

Romans 8:15–17

For ye have not received the spirit of bondage again to fear; but ye have received the Spirit of adoption, whereby we cry, Abba, Father. The Spirit itself beareth witness with our spirit, that we are the children of

God: and if children, then heirs; heirs of God, and joint-heirs with Christ; if so be that we suffer with him, that we may be also glorified together.

Now think about it.

When you trusted Christ and Christ alone for your salvation, you did not receive any kind of spirit that would make you a slave to fear, or make you feel like you were in bondage to a set of rules and regulations you knew you could never keep, but instead you received the Spirit of adoption by whom we cry out as needy young children, "Abba, Father." The Holy Spirit of God Himself testifies (the testimony of a truthful witness under oath giving clear evidence to our spirit) that we are dearly loved children of God, and since we are God's children, then we are also His heirs—heirs of God and joint heirs with Christ (which means we will inherit some of the joys of His glory and honor in the future but presupposes that we will also inherit some of His suffering in the present).

How can this affect me?

It is hard to see yourself as a slave to fear and a child of God at the same time. Slaves obey because they have to; children obey because they want to. Slaves are motivated by fear of punishment; children are motivated by assurance of love. Slaves are considered a thing to be bought, sold, used, and abused. Children are a part of a family to be loved, nourished, protected, and provided for. Slaves can be purchased. Children can be adopted. Slaves live in fear under the hand of an evil slave master; children live in joy under the hand of a father that wants only the best for them. Slaves never feel a part of a family and wonder when they will be gotten rid of; adopted children know they have been chosen to be a part of a family forever. Slaves sing of bondage and mistreatment; adopted children sing of hope and joy. Believer, be encouraged that you are a child of God! What an incredible, undeserved joy . . . to be a child of God! Meditate on these words by Ron Hamilton:

I am adopted; I'm a child of the King.
God is my Father, and He owns ev'rything.
He walks beside me; He's my very best friend.
Praise God, I'll never be lonely again.
I'm adopted, hallelujah! I've got a new song.
I'm adopted, hallelujah! I fin'lly belong.
I've got a brand new family overflowing with love.
I'm a child of my Father above.

("I'm Adopted," *Majesty Hymns*)

14

MEDITATION 3

■ ■ ■

FEAR FEARS JOY!

This is what God says.

Acts 20:22–24

And now, behold, I go bound in the spirit unto Jerusalem, not knowing the things that shall befall me there: save that the Holy Ghost witnesseth in every city, saying that bonds and afflictions abide me. But none of these things move me, neither count I my life dear unto myself, so that I might finish my course with joy, and the ministry, which I have received of the Lord Jesus, to testify the gospel of the grace of God.

Now think about it.

Paul, addressing the elders and leaders of the church in Ephesus said, "Listen, please, because this is very important for you to hear. Right now God's Spirit is working in my heart compelling me to go to Jerusalem as soon as possible (I hope by the day of Pentecost) even though I do not know what will happen to me there (it is very possible that I may be killed). I do know that in every city I now enter, the Holy Spirit warns me that I will face afflictions, beatings, persecution, and possibly prison. But none of these things (not pain, not suffering, not imprisonment, not one of these) move me to quit, cause me to fear, or motivate me to give up; neither do I count my life dear unto myself (I do not value my own life and I am not afraid to die). I want to finish the race God has asked me to run and complete the ministry God has given me. I want to finish my course (the precious ministry of sharing the gospel of the grace of God) with joy! The inner joy only God can give must take the place of any fear, worry, and apprehension in my heart. If I keep my focus off my own afflictions and keep it on my Lord and those that need to hear the precious gospel of God's grace, I can and will complete this task with joy.

How can this affect me?

Fear's greatest enemy is joy. Worry's strongest opponent is joy. Apprehension, anxiety, and paralyzing concern cannot conquer true, biblical joy. It was joy that motivated Paul to keep going even when he knew afflictions were waiting for him in the next town he entered. It was joy that encouraged Paul to keep preaching even though he could feel the sharp edge of the soldier's whip cutting into the flesh of his back. It was joy that prodded Paul even though his next night's sleep would probably be in a dark, dank prison cell. Fear fears joy. Worry worries when joy takes control of a heart. Apprehension is very apprehensive when it is called to attack a Spirit-filled, joyful servant of God. Fear is motivated by what others think; joy is motivated by what God thinks. Worry is consumed by what terrible thing might happen; joy is encouraged and content with what a sovereign God wills to happen. Fear and joy are great enemies. One comes from God and the other does not. Which would you rather have control your life?

This is what God says.

Joel 2:21

Fear not, O land; be glad and rejoice: for the Lord will do great things.

Now think about it.

Fear not. Don't be afraid, O land, which is made of nothing more than dirt, ground, earth, and clay; be glad and rejoice for the Lord will do great things.

How can this affect me?

The land promised to Abraham was land—land that God would bless—but still made of nothing more than rock, sand, and clay. Have you ever felt worthless as dirt? Interestingly enough, God directed some of His promises to something as trivial and cheap as dirt. Through the prophet Joel, God told the ground (plain old mud and clay) that He was going to do great things for it. Maybe He was promising this parched earth what He promised the ground in another part of the middle east through the prophet Isaiah when He said, "The wilderness and the solitary place shall be glad for them; and the desert shall rejoice, and blossom as the rose. It shall blossom abundantly, and rejoice even with joy and singing: the glory of Lebanon shall be given unto it, the excellency of Carmel and Sharon, they shall see the glory of the Lord, and the excellency of our God." If something as worthless as dirt and rocks can rejoice with joy and singing (not to be confused with any form of rock music), can rejoice in seeing God's magnificent glory, and can rejoice as it views the excellency of God, why can't we? If God can make a rose bloom out of the desert soil, He can certainly put a smile on a face hardened with grief. If God can make the massive cedars of Lebanon grow from worthless soil, He can produce fruit in our lives, even love, joy, and peace! At whatever point you think you are worthless, insignificant, useless, and of no value to God or others, look down on the ground you walk on. Study the dirt! If God promised the earth He would do *great things*, cannot

■ ■ ■

THE LORD WILL DO GREAT THINGS.

■ ■ ■

He do the same for you? God told the demon-filled wild man of Gadera, "Go home to your friends and tell them how *great things* the Lord has done for you, and had compassion on you." The young mother of Jesus said, "For He has done to me *great things*, and holy is His name." David was so overwhelmed with the *great things* God did for him that he repeated it twice in Psalm 126. "Then was our mouth filled with laughter, and our tongue with singing: then said they among the heathen, The Lord hath done *great things* for them. The Lord hath done *great things* for us; whereof we are glad." If God did such *great things* for David, Mary, and the dirt, cannot He do the same for you? Rejoice and be glad. Fear not. Don't be afraid. You serve a God who can do *great things*!

MEDITATION 4

■ ■ ■

MY GOD IS BIGGER THAN YOUR FEAR.

This is what God says.

Hebrews 2:14–15

Forasmuch then as the children are partakers of flesh and blood, he also himself likewise took part of the same; that through death he might destroy him that had the power of death, that is, the devil; and deliver them who through fear of death were all their lifetime subject to bondage.

Now think about it.

Therefore, since all believers (all God's children) are made of flesh and blood, our Lord Jesus Christ Himself shared in their humanity by taking on the same kind of physical body that they had, so that through His death, He would destroy and render powerless he who had the power of death, that is, the Devil, and rescue, deliver, and free those who all their lifetime (for their entire lives) were held in bondage and slavery by their fear of death.

How can this affect me?

Do you fear death? Are you afraid to die? Is it the process of death that scares you or death itself? Are you terrified with the thought of dying? Christ ripped the one weapon that made the Devil so powerful right out of his hand—death. Satan knows that if he can keep men in their sin until they die, he has them. His goal is through death to keep men separated from God for eternity. God attacked death and the Devil with a stronger weapon than death itself—eternal life. Christ's resurrection defeated death once and for all. For Christ to defeat death by rising from the dead, He first had to die. Jesus destroyed death and all its consequences. Believer, you don't have to fear death but can now actually look forward to it. Like Paul did! He said that to die was "gain" and that death was "far better" than living! To his Corinthian friends he wrote, "O death where is your sting? O grave, where is your victory?" Before salvation, many are enslaved to the terror of the afterlife.

For the Christian, physical death is actually a continuation of his eternal life. To God, the death of His saints is a precious thing because at death, they are immediately ushered into His presence. No believer should be a slave to the fear of death. Believer, you have been freed!

This is what God says.

Psalm 62:7–8

In God is my salvation and my glory: the rock of my strength, and my refuge, is in God. Trust in him at all times; ye people, pour out your heart before him: God is a refuge for us. Selah.

Now think about it.

In God and God only I find my salvation (I cannot save myself but am thankful for a God Who saved me) and my glory (I am nothing in myself but am honored by my God): the rock of my strength (I am weak but my God will strengthen me) and my refuge (I am insecure but my God protects me) is in God. Trust in Him (I far too often trust in myself) at all times (I far too often choose when I will trust in God); O people, pour out your heart before Him (I far too often keep all my hurts and heartaches inside and refuse to pray): God is a refuge for us (I far too often forget that God is always available for me to run to, to depend on, and to trust in). Selah (I will now pause and take the time necessary to let these great truths about my great God sink into my heart).

How can this affect me?

When there is a storm outside showing its intensity with lightning bolts that streak through the dark clouds and thunder that roars and shakes people in their boots, there is no safer place for a small child than "in" the house and "in" a parent's arms. The comforting hug by mom does not change the intensity of the storm, and the secure feeling of dad's arms does not lessen the thunder or the lightning. The security and comfort of depending on someone who not only loves you but is so much bigger and more powerful than you makes the storm on the outside almost nonexistent.

The psalmist (who personally knew how to fear and worry) starts and ends verse 7 with the words "in God," picturing Him as our secret cave or private refuge. It is a place of safety and security that only God and you know the path to. No problem on earth or power in the universe can force you out of that refuge. It is safe. It is secure. The path to this secure refuge is found by those marked with utter desperation and total dependence on God.

- You cannot divide your dependence between you and God.

- You must trust Him at all times.

- You cannot choose when you want to trust.

- You must trust Him at all times.

- You cannot get distracted or weary and fall back on your fearful worrying again.

- You must trust Him at all times.

- You cannot view "trust in God" as an item on a dinner smorgasbord to take if you like it but leave it if you don't.

- You must trust Him at all times.

- You must desperately pour out your heart to God. Don't hold it all in just to cry it out on a sleepless night.

- Pour out your heart to God.

- Don't just pray through your surface problems.

- Pour out your heart to God.
- Don't think that nobody cares.
- Pour out your heart to God.
- Don't hold back your anguish or hold in your turmoil.
- Pour out your heart to God.
- God is your salvation and your glory,
- God is the rock of your strength,
- God is your refuge, and He is your God.
- Trust in Him at all times;
- Pour out your heart before Him;
- God is your refuge.

Now stop and meditate on this for a while. Selah.

MEDITATION 5

■ ■ ■

STICKS AND STONES WILL BREAK MY BONES, BUT WORDS WILL NEVER "SCARE" ME.

This is what God says.

Nehemiah 6:10–16

Afterward I came unto the house of Shemaiah the son of Delaiah the son of Mehetabeel, who was shut up; and he said, Let us meet together in the house of God, within the temple, and let us shut the doors of the temple: for they will come to slay thee; yea, in the night will they come to slay thee. And I said, Should such a man as I flee? and who is there, that, being as I am, would go into the temple to save his life? I will not go in. And, lo, I perceived that God had not sent him; but that he pronounced this prophecy against me: for Tobiah and Sanballat had hired him. Therefore was he hired, that I should be afraid, and do so, and sin, and that they might have matter for an evil report, that they might reproach me. My God, think thou upon Tobiah and Sanballat according to these their works, and on the prophetess Noadiah, and the rest of the prophets, that would have put me in fear. So the wall was finished in the twenty and fifth day of the month Elul, in fifty and two days. And it came to pass, that when all our enemies heard thereof, and all the heathen that were about us saw these things, they were much cast down in their own eyes: for they perceived that this work was wrought of our God.

Now think about it.

Nehemiah said, "When I entered into the house of Shemaiah, the son of Delaiah, the grandson of Mehetabeel, who was shut up and confined in his own home, he said to me, 'We need to hide in the house of God, inside the temple, where we can shut the doors of the temple so no one can find us, because your enemies are coming to kill you; in the night (maybe even tonight) they will come to kill you!'" Then I said to Shemaiah, "Should a man like me run? Do you think I would be so selfish to go into the temple to save my own life? No way! I will not go in." Then I perceived that he was not sent by God but that he pronounced this prophecy against me because my enemies, Tobiah and Sanballat, had hired him to lie to me. He was hired to scare me and cause me to be afraid for my own life, and if I sinned by not trusting God and running into the temple to hide, they would then have an evil report against me and use it to reproach me and discredit my leadership. Then I prayed, "My God, remember the lies and deceit of Tobiah and Sanballat and how they tried to intimidate me and cause me to fear. Remember also the prophetess Noadiah, and the rest of the prophets, who have tried to put me in fear, frighten me, and make me quit!" Even though our enemies attempted to frighten and intimidate us, the wall was finished in the twenty-fifth day of the month Elul, in just fifty-two days. When all our enemies heard that the wall was completed, and all the surrounding, unbelieving nations saw what God (through His people) had accomplished, the same ones that attempted to frighten us were incredibly afraid and cast down in their own eyes, which resulted in a loss of all their confidence. Why? They perceived and saw that this work was accomplished only with the help of Israel's almighty, all-powerful God.

How can this affect me?

Those who attempt to cause others to fear are often fearful people. They may not fear us, but they do fear our God. Even though they think that we can be intimidated, they know they cannot intimidate God. Sanballat and Tobiah ganged up on Nehemiah. Isn't it interesting that those who seek to pressure you to sin or compromise never fight alone? Most intimidators never sing solos; they like the security of a choir. Even Goliath had another soldier carrying a shield with him when he was confronted by David. You may at times think you are in the minority, but with God you are always in the majority. With God on your side you do not need to fear any man or any group of men. They are only tough when they are successful at intimidating others to give in. The second someone boldly stands up against them they back down. Many intimidators are easily intimidated. A proud "strong-man" is tough only as long as someone tougher does not show up. Those who intimidate, mock, and try to embarrass believers forget that an attack on a Christian is actually an attack on that Christian's God. The only ones who think they are big and God is small are those who do not know God. I assume that since you are reading this book, you know God. Like Nehemiah, the more you know about God the less you will fear man. The more you trust God the less you'll fear. The more you depend on God's protection, the less you will fearfully attempt to manipulate your life. Instead of running and hiding, Nehemiah called their bluff, said NO and kept doing what he knew God wanted him to do. Do you want to defeat the fear of intimidation? Say NO! Do what God has called you to do with the confidence that Nehemiah had. Even though Nehemiah's enemies attempted to frighten and intimidate him, the wall was finished. When all his enemies heard that the wall was completed, and all the surrounding,

> THE MORE YOU TRUST GOD THE LESS YOU'LL FEAR.

unbelieving nations saw what God (through His people) had accomplished, the same ones that attempted to frighten them were incredibly afraid and cast down in their own eyes, which resulted in a loss of all their confidence. Why? They perceived and saw that this work was accomplished only with the help of Israel's almighty, all-powerful God. Don't be afraid of what others say about you. Don't fear their sticks, stones, or words. Someday they will see that what was accomplished in your life was accomplished through the hands of an almighty, all-powerful God.

This is what God says.

John 13:36–14:3

Simon Peter said unto him, Lord, whither goest thou? Jesus answered him, Whither I go, thou canst not follow me now; but thou shalt follow me afterwards. Peter said unto him, Lord, why cannot I follow thee now? I will lay down my life for thy sake. Jesus answered him, Wilt thou lay down thy life for my sake? Verily, verily, I say unto thee, The cock shall not crow, till thou hast denied me thrice. Let not your heart be troubled: ye believe in God, believe also in me. In my Father's house are many mansions: if it were not so, I would have told you. I go to prepare a place for you. And if I go and prepare a place for you, I will come again, and receive you unto myself; that where I am, there ye may be also.

Now think about it.

Simon Peter: "Lord, where are You going?"

Jesus Christ: "Where I am going, you cannot follow Me right now, but you will follow Me afterwards."

Simon Peter: "Lord, why can't I follow You now? I will lay down my life for Your sake!"

Jesus Christ: "Will you lay down your life for My sake? Peter, here is the truth. The rooster will not crow announcing that morning is here until you have denied Me three times. But, Peter, don't fear. Don't let your heart be troubled or saddened. Believe in God. Believe also in Me. In My Father's house are many rooms and dwelling places (dwelling places even for those who have denied Me like you). If this were not true, do you think I would have told you that I am going to prepare a place for you? And if I go and prepare a place for you, I will come again, and take you with Me, that where I am, you will be also."

How can this affect me?

You have to wonder if the first-century alarm clock (the crowing of a rooster) daily reminded Peter of this very conversation. His confidence and character were being questioned. He knew the strength of an iron will but was not yet educated in the power of a fearful heart. His self-confidence stood shocked at the next-day prophecy coming from the lips of his Lord. He? Peter? The leader of these rugged followers of Christ? Deny his Lord? Never! What could ever make him turn his back on Christ? He had already given up his fishing business so it wouldn't be money. He was happily married so it wouldn't be another woman. He was chosen to be in the inner circle with Jesus Christ, the Messiah, the Son of God, so it wouldn't be pride or fame that would cause such a denial. What could it be? Peter had yet to face the dreadful, manipulating power of fear. No one would say he lacked bravery because he was brave enough to pull a sword in the face of an angry mob in the garden of Gethsemane. He couldn't be accused of lacking courage because he had the courage to follow the soldiers who took Christ to a religious leader's courtyard to be mocked and questioned. Then it happened. Right after a soldier slapped Jesus across the face, a young servant girl asked Peter if he knew Jesus of Nazareth—he said that he didn't. Right after they bound Jesus' hands like a criminal, Peter was asked if he was the one with the sword in Gethsemane that stood up for Christ—again

Peter denied. At this point a prophetic sound pierced that dark night—a rooster crowed. And every crow of every rooster from that time forward could have reminded Peter of two things: the fearful cowardice of his wicked heart and the future comfort of living with his forgiving Lord. As Peter bitterly wept over the fear that caused him to turn on the very Son of God, his heart must have been comforted as he remembered the promise of Jesus, "Peter, don't let your heart be troubled. You have got to believe Me. I am going to prepare a place in My house for you to live with Me . . . forever. I know you denied Me, but I forgave you. I know you were overcome with fear, but My eternal love for you will overcome your fear. Peter, you learned a very important lesson that I want all who love Me to learn. When you are weak, then I am strong. I did not choose to love you because of what you can do for Me, but for what I can do for you. Don't be troubled. Don't fear. Give Me some time to finish your place in my Father's house; then I will come back to get you. I promise."

MEDITATION 6

■ ■ ■

LIFE IS FEARFUL, HANDLE WITH PRAYER.

This is what God says.

Exodus 14:10, 13–14

And when Pharaoh drew nigh, the children of Israel lifted up their eyes, and, behold, the Egyptians marched after them; and they were sore afraid: and the children of Israel cried out unto the Lord. . . . And Moses said unto the people, Fear ye not, stand still, and see the salvation of the Lord, which he will shew to you to day: for the Egyptians whom ye have seen to day, ye shall see them again no more for ever. The Lord shall fight for you, and ye shall hold your peace.

Now think about it.

When Pharaoh and his entire army of battle chariots, trained horsemen, and bloodthirsty foot soldiers drew near to the fleeing Israelite families, the children of Israel looked back and saw the Egyptian army coming after them. Knowing what would happen when they were caught and sent back to Egypt (if they were not slaughtered right there in the desert), they were hopelessly frightened. The children of Israel cried out unto the Lord in fear, doubt, and angry complaints. . . . Then Moses said to the frightened people, "Fear not! Don't be afraid! Stand back and today you will see the Lord save you and deliver you from the hand of the Egyptians. I promise you, you will never, ever see them alive again. The Lord will fight for you and silence your fear and doubts."

How can this affect me?

There are times when life frightens us (maybe not as frightening as an angry army seeking to slaughter us). There are times when difficulties will push us into a corner with nowhere to turn and no way to escape (maybe not as impossible as an uncrossable Red Sea). There are times when hardships will be so consuming that all hope disappears (maybe not as hopeless as what the children of Israel faced being pinned between an oceanlike sea and an Egyptian army). It is during these frightening, impossible, hopeless times that we too will see God's deliverance! How? I don't know. When? I have no idea. But God will get us through. Israel saw absolutely no way out of their situation. How is it possible to escape being penned in between a huge sea and a barbarian army? "With men it is impossible, but not with God: for with God all things are possible" (Mark 10:27). What happened to Israel that fright-filled day? As Paul Harvey would put it, "And now, the rest of the story. . . ."

> And Moses stretched out his hand over the sea; and the Lord caused the sea to go back by a strong east wind all that night, and made the sea dry land, and the waters were divided. And the children of Israel went into the midst of the sea upon the dry ground: and the waters were a wall unto them on their right hand, and on their left. And the Egyptians pursued, and went in after them to the midst of the sea, even all Pharaoh's horses, his chariots, and his horsemen. And it came to pass, that in the morning watch the Lord looked unto the host of the Egyptians through the pillar of fire and of the cloud, and troubled the host of the Egyptians, and took off their chariot wheels, that they drave them heavily: so that the Egyptians said, Let us flee from the face of Israel; for the Lord fighteth for them against the Egyptians.

And the Lord said unto Moses, Stretch out thine hand over the sea, that the waters may come again upon the Egyptians, upon their chariots, and upon their horsemen. And Moses stretched forth his hand over the sea, and the sea returned to his strength when the morning appeared; and the Egyptians fled against it; and the Lord overthrew the Egyptians in the midst of the sea. And the waters returned, and covered the chariots, and the horsemen, and all the host of Pharaoh that came into the sea after them; there remained not so much as one of them. But the children of Israel walked upon dry land in the midst of the sea; and the waters were a wall unto them on their right hand, and on their left. Thus the Lord saved Israel that day out of the hand of the Egyptians; and Israel saw the Egyptians dead upon the sea shore. And Israel saw that great work which the Lord did upon the Egyptians: and the people feared the Lord, and believed the Lord, and his servant Moses. (Exodus 14:21–31)

It was a miracle. It was an impossible deliverance from an all-possible God. God has delivered before and will deliver again. Trust Him. Believe Him. Fear Him. And remember, with man, many things are impossible. But with God . . . nothing, absolutely nothing is impossible!

This is what God says.

2 Chronicles 32:7–8

Be strong and courageous, be not afraid nor dismayed for the king of Assyria, nor for all the multitude that is with him: for there be more with us than with him: with him is an arm of flesh; but with us is the Lord our God to help us, and to fight our battles. And the people rested themselves upon the words of Hezekiah king of Judah.

Now think about it.

Be strong and courageous; do not be afraid, dismayed, or discouraged because of Sennacherib, king of Assyria, neither because of the huge hoard, the vast army, or the multitude of soldiers that are with him: for actually, we have a power that he does not have; we have the advantage because the One with us is greater than the one with him: all he has with him is the arm of flesh, nothing more; but with us is the almighty, all-powerful Lord our God! He will help us. He will fight our battles. And the people rested on the encouraging words of King Hezekiah with such reliance that confidence gave way to fear.

How can this affect me?

The people rested upon the words of King Hezekiah. The people relied on the words of King Hezekiah. The people were reassured by the words of King Hezekiah. The people were strengthened by the words of King Hezekiah. The people gained confidence from the words of King Hezekiah. What caused such unrest, weakness, lack of confidence, and fear in King Hezekiah's people? Who threatened their security and safety? Why did King Hezekiah and his confidant, the prophet Isaiah, cry out in prayer to heaven for wisdom, strength, and protection? It all centered on the very powerful King Sennacherib, who marched through the neighboring countries destroying everyone who stood against him. King Sennacherib had God's people surrounded and was just waiting for the kill. Read the account from 2 Chronicles 32 to get a good picture of why these people needed confidence, strength, and protection from God.

> After these things, and the establishment thereof, Sennacherib king of Assyria came, and entered into Judah, and encamped against the fenced cities, and thought to win them for himself. And when Hezekiah saw that Sennacherib was

come, and that he was purposed to fight against Jerusalem, he took counsel with his princes and his mighty men to stop the waters of the fountains which were without the city: and they did help him. So there was gathered much people together, who stopped all the fountains, and the brook that ran through the midst of the land, saying, Why should the kings of Assyria come, and find much water? Also he strengthened himself, and built up all the wall that was broken, and raised it up to the towers, and another wall without, and repaired Millo in the city of David, and made darts [arrows] and shields in abundance. And he set captains of war over the people, and gathered them together to him in the street of the gate of the city, and spake comfortably to them, saying, Be strong and courageous, be not afraid nor dismayed for the king of Assyria, nor for all the multitude that is with him: for there be more with us than with him: with him is an arm of flesh; but with us is the Lord our God to help us, and to fight our battles. And the people rested themselves upon the words of Hezekiah king of Judah.

After this did Sennacherib king of Assyria send his servants to Jerusalem, (but he himself laid siege against Lachish, and all his power with him,) unto Hezekiah king of Judah, and unto all Judah that were at Jerusalem, saying, Thus saith Sennacherib king of Assyria, Whereon do ye trust, that ye abide in the siege in Jerusalem? Doth not

Hezekiah persuade you to give over yourselves to die by famine and by thirst, saying, The Lord our God shall deliver us out of the hand of the king of Assyria? Hath not the same Hezekiah taken away his high places and his altars, and commanded Judah and Jerusalem, saying, Ye shall worship before one altar, and burn incense upon it? Know ye not what I and my fathers have done unto all the people of other lands? were the gods of the nations of those lands any ways able to deliver their lands out of mine hand? Who was there among all the gods of those nations that my fathers utterly destroyed, that could deliver his people out of mine hand, that your God should be able to deliver you out of mine hand? Now therefore let not Hezekiah deceive you, nor persuade you on this manner, neither yet believe him: for no god of any nation or kingdom was able to deliver his people out of mine hand, and out of the hand of my fathers: how much less shall your God deliver you out of mine hand? And his servants spake yet more against the Lord God, and against his servant Hezekiah. He wrote also letters to rail on the Lord God of Israel, and to speak against him, saying, As the gods of the nations of other lands have not delivered their people out of mine hand, so shall not the God of Hezekiah deliver his people out of mine hand. Then they cried with a loud voice in the Jews' speech unto the people of Jerusalem that were on the wall, to affright them, and to trouble them; that they might take the city. And they spake against the God of Jerusalem, as against the gods of the people of the earth, which were the work of the hands of man. (2 Chronicles 32:1–19)

Sennacherib looked invincible. Hezekiah and Isaiah knew differently as was evident by their response to this wicked king's attack on God and God's people.

And for this cause Hezekiah the king, and the prophet Isaiah the son of Amoz, prayed and cried to heaven. (2 Chronicles 32:20)

God quickly and quietly answered the prayer of Isaiah and Hezekiah.

And the Lord sent an angel, which cut off all the mighty men of valour, and the leaders and captains in the camp of the king of Assyria. So he [King Sennacherib] returned with shame of face to his own land. And when he was come into the house of his god, they that came forth of his own bowels slew him there with the sword. Thus the Lord saved Hezekiah and the inhabitants of Jerusalem from the hand of Sennacherib the king of Assyria, and from the hand of all other, and guided them on every side. (2 Chronicles 32:21–22)

What could be considered the "Sennacherib" in your life? What or who is attempting to shift your confidence in and focus off the Lord and on the fearful pressures or antagonists that surround you? Sennacherib set a siege around Jerusalem, thinking he could starve or scare these people into defeat. Is there any sin, struggle, or stress that is surrounding your heart and life in such a way that you almost feel choked off of any hope for victory? After they had prepared for battle and done everything possible to stand against the enemy (still without confident hope for victory), what did the prophet Isaiah and King Hezekiah then do? They cried out to the Lord! When you are surrounded by fear and anxiety, do you cry out to the Lord? Did God answer the cry of these faithful leaders? He delivered and saved His people and in doing so totally destroyed the enemy. Will he not answer your cry in the same way? Fearful? Then simply cry out to your Lord.

This is what God says.

Philippians 1:27–30

Only let your conversation be as it becometh the gospel of Christ: that whether I come and see you, or else be absent, I may hear of your affairs, that ye stand fast in one spirit, with one mind striving together for the faith of the gospel; and in nothing terrified by your adversaries: which is to them an evident token of perdition, but to you of salvation, and that of God. For unto you it is given in the behalf of Christ, not only to believe on him, but also to suffer for his sake; having the same conflict which ye saw in me, and now hear to be in me.

Now think about it.

Only let your life, your daily conduct, your consistent lifestyle that others are watching, make the gospel of Christ attractive, appealing, delightful, and desirable to others. Then, whether I come to see you or hear about you in my absence, I will know that you are encouraging each other with the same mind and spirit to stand firm. Stand firm as one man, unmovable, and unshakeable for the faith of the gospel without in any way being frightened, seriously alarmed, or overly concerned by those who hate you and oppose you. When those who hate you see your commitment to stand together for what you believe no matter how terrible the persecution becomes, it is a sign to them (even proof) of their own destruction; at the same time it gives you the assurance of your salvation, the proof that you are saved and that your salvation comes from God and God alone. For as a Christian, it has been granted to you, on behalf of

Christ, not only to believe on Him, but also to suffer for His sake, experiencing the very same conflict that you saw me experience and now hear that I am experiencing again.

How can this affect me?

You are being watched! Whether you know it or not, your life is under examination. People examine the power of the gospel message by examining your lifestyle. A lifestyle (conversation) consumed with faith, trust, and total confidence in God makes God and His gospel message look very attractive. A life filled with worry, fear, and anxiety actually makes God look like an uncaring, distant, and even impotent God. If your family sees you paralyzed by fear, they have to conclude that you do not believe that God is all-powerful. If your friends see your worry, they will know that you are not trusting in an almighty God. Worry and fear do nothing to make the gospel attractive, delightful, or appealing to others. When unbelievers are successful in frightening and terrifying you through their malicious words and hateful attitudes, they are successful in proclaiming their hateful message that God is not the wonderful, wise, caring God that His Word declares. We can keep the gospel looking good when we replace fear with confidence, worry with trust, and apprehension with faith. Your fears affect not only the way others see you but also the way others see your God!

This is what God says.

Luke 18:1

And he spake a parable unto them to this end, that men ought always to pray, and not to faint.

Now think about it.

And Jesus spake a parable unto them to this end (Jesus took a life-changing truth and explained and illustrated it in story form to make sure His listeners totally understood what was being said. This same life-changing truth He had Luke write down for you and me to read, understand, and obey.)

"At all times
we ought to pray
and not lose heart."

How can this affect me?

Most people love a good story. And no story can be considered a "good" story unless the final paragraph begins with the classic words "the moral of the story is. . . ." Luke 18 gave us Jesus' story to illustrate and demonstrate the biblical truth of continual, fervent, effective prayer.

> There was in a city a judge, which feared not God, neither regarded man: and there was a widow in that city; and she came unto him saying, Avenge me of mine adversary. And he would not for a while: but afterward he said within himself, Though I fear not God, nor regard man; yet because this widow troubleth me, I will avenge her, lest by her continual coming she weary me. And the Lord saith, Hear what the unjust judge saith. And shall not God avenge His own elect, which cry day and night unto him, though he bear long with them? I tell you that He will avenge them speedily.

Here is a city judge who can receive no personal gain from this situation, has no morals that would dictate his decisions, and does not fear future judgment from any supreme being. If a guy like this, without any internal motivation, will answer a poor widow's request and give her what she needs, will not God be just and fair and give to those whom He loves and protects if they will consistently and persistently ask Him? If you think God is not listening to your requests, don't faint, don't lose heart; God is listening and wanting you to demonstrate your trust in Him by your continual asking. Every time you ask God for anything, you are evidencing faith in your heart. It is the faith that pleases God. God inspired Luke to include this parable in his Gospel to keep us from losing heart. God is pleased with persistent, continual faith. As the following verses admonish us, pray and don't lose heart.

Luke 21:36

Watch ye therefore, and pray always, that ye may be accounted worthy to escape all these things that shall come to pass, and to stand before the Son of man.

Romans 12:12

Rejoicing in hope; patient in tribulation; continuing instant in prayer.

Ephesians 6:18

Praying always with all prayer and supplication in the Spirit, and watching thereunto with all perseverance and supplication for all saints.

Colossians 4:2

Continue in prayer, and watch in the same with thanksgiving.

1 Thessalonians 5:17–18

Pray without ceasing. In every thing give thanks: for this is the will of God in Christ Jesus concerning you.

MEDITATION 7

■ ■ ■

FEARFUL WORRIERS DO NOT KNOW GOD VERY WELL.

This is what God says.

Ezekiel 2:6–8

And thou, son of man, be not afraid of them, neither be afraid of their words, though briers and thorns be with thee, and thou dost dwell among scorpions: be not afraid of their words, nor be dismayed at their looks, though they be a rebellious house. And thou shalt speak my words unto them, whether they will hear, or whether they will forbear: for they are most rebellious. But thou, son of man, hear what I say unto thee; Be not thou rebellious like that rebellious house: open thy mouth, and eat that I give thee.

Now think about it.

Ezekiel, do not be afraid of the stubborn and rebellious people I have sent you to help. Do not be afraid of their words and what they say about you both to your face and behind your back. Serving these people will not be much different from fighting your way through a briar patch where thorns and thistles reach out, rip your clothes, and gouge into your skin. It will hurt just as much. Speaking to such rebels will bring no less pain than the sting of a scorpion you might accidentally step on. I remind you again, do not be afraid of their words. Don't be dismayed, troubled, or offended at the way they look at you even though their hard, obstinate hearts will be obvious by their hardened, mean, and condescending countenances. Ezekiel, no matter how scary it gets, I want you to speak My words to them. I will tell you what to say even though they will not like it. Keep telling them the truth, My truth, whether they will listen or not (by the way, these people are so rebellious they probably won't listen). Ezekiel, don't get caught up in what you are preaching against; listen to what I say to you. Don't you become rebellious like those you are trying to persuade. I will tell you only what is best for them and for you. I will deal with you like a young mother who feeds her baby. She does not always give her child what he likes or wants but what he needs. Ezekiel, open your mouth and eat everything I put on your plate.

How can this affect me?

We need to let God fix our plates. Most of us stay away from anyone and anything that can hurt us or bring fear into our lives. We would not choose to put ourselves in what appears to be a no-win situation. We would avoid our fears (like speaking in public or facing people who totally disagree with us) rather than face them. On the other hand, God does not seem to lead us away from fearful experiences but wants to encourage us through them. We had better allow God to fix our plates in life rather than choose from the smorgasbord of selfishness from which most of us feed. When God is preparing the menu, there will be a whole lot more spinach, broccoli, brussels sprouts, and red beets than french fires, hamburgers, and milkshakes. God does not always give us what we want, but He will always give us what we need. When God burdens us to do something that we would rather not do (puts something on our plate that we would rather not eat), we cannot gripe, complain, or respond with "I don't like that!" We must be committed to doing His will until God changes our hearts by changing our likes. Once we taste God's protection and power in a troubling circumstance, God creates in us an appetite and a hunger that is satisfied only by trusting Him more and more. The more we experience God's supernatural power in overcoming fear, the more we enjoy leaning on His wisdom and grace. "O taste and see that the Lord is good." Accept what God serves you and you will be amazed in your renewed ability to serve Him.

This is what God says.

Luke 19:20–23

And another came, saying, Lord, behold, here is thy pound, which I have kept laid up in a napkin: for I feared thee, because thou art an austere man: thou takest up that thou layedst not down, and reapest that thou didst not sow. And he saith unto him, Out of thine own mouth will I judge thee, thou wicked servant. Thou knewest that I was an austere man, taking up that I laid not down, and reaping that I did not sow: wherefore then gavest not thou my money into the bank, that at my coming I might have required mine own with usury?

Now think about it.

The third of three servants that were asked to manage some of his master's money came to his master saying, "Here is every penny that you gave me. I hid it in my apron so I wouldn't have to be bothered with it, but I wasn't expecting you back so soon. And just so you know, the reason I didn't do anything with your money was that I feared you. I was afraid of you. I know that you are a hard, demanding, and austere man. You take what is not really yours and reap what you didn't sow." Then his master said to him, "I will be fair to you and judge you according to what you just said. You should be afraid. You are a wicked, selfish servant! You should fear. Not only are you too lazy to do what you were asked, but you obviously have not spent much time getting to know me very well. My true servants know that I am honest, fair, and good. You said that I was a hard, demanding, and austere man who takes what is not mine and reaps what I didn't sow. I am not that kind of master. Why didn't you simply put my money into the bank so that when I returned, I

HE PROMISES
TO SUPPLY ALL
OUR NEEDS.

would have at least withdrawn my money with interest? You should be afraid.

How can this affect me?

How well do you know God? The third servant obviously did not know his master very well. He accused him of things that were totally against his character. We fear because we do not know God very well. Those who fear financial problems have never taken the time to learn that God helps us with our financial pressures by teaching us that godliness with contentment is great gain; that we brought nothing into this world, and it is certain we can carry nothing out; and that if all we have is food and clothing, we should be content. He also promises to supply all our needs according to His riches, which are incalculable. Why fear with a God like that? Those who fear the future have never learned that God's mercies are new every morning; that God sets our steps in an orderly fashion before us through His Word and strengthens us against life-dominating sins; and that if we simply trust in Him with all our hearts, He will direct our paths. Why fear with a God like that? Those who fear rejection either do not know or forget that we are to cast every care we have on God because He cares so much for us; they forget that God does not love us with a conditional love based on our behavior or performance; and they forget that God's thoughts of us are far more than we can even imagine. Why fear with a God like that? The more you fear, the less you know God. Attack your fears by studying the character of God. God protects. God provides. God passionately loves. Why fear with a God like that?

This is what God says.

1 Peter 5:6–7
Humble yourselves therefore under the mighty hand of God, that he may exalt you in due time: casting all your care upon him; for he careth for you.

Now think about it.

Because God opposes the proud and arrogant but gives His undeserved grace to the humble, humble yourself under the mighty hand of God so that at the proper time, God will exalt you and lift you up. Place all your anxieties, cares, and worries in God's mighty hands because you know that He cares for you, loves you more than you deserve, and has the power to take care of every difficult situation you face.

How can this affect me?

Who cares about your cares? Who cares about your worries? Who cares about your anxieties? Who cares about the fears and failures that are literally pulling you apart? Who cares? Most people have so many worries and cares stuffed in their pockets they don't have any room for the cares of others. So who cares? Most people are so overwhelmed and exasperated with their own panic-driven lives they cannot even conceive of taking on anyone else's problems. So who cares? Most friends are powerless to do anything about their own anxieties and therefore cannot reach out any farther than their own noses to help anyone else. So who cares? It will have to be someone who has no worries of his own, who has his own life in total control, and who has the power and ability to do something about your cares! Do you know anyone like that? When your cares are pulling your mind, will, and emotions in every direction imaginable, God is there to help you pull yourself back together. When your heart is so distracted by problems that you cannot focus on what and who really matters, God is there to help you regain your focus on Him. When the burden of your fears becomes so heavy that you are just about ready to buckle under its pressure, God is there waiting for you to heave that burden off your back and onto His shoulders. Why? Why would God want to take your problems off you and place them on Himself? Because He "cares" for you! When God tells us to be "careful" (full of care) for nothing, He is introducing to us a bad kind of care. There is "good care" and "bad care." We are professionals at dealing with the "bad care," which is seen in our worries, our anxieties, our fears, and our apprehensions. God's kind of care is a "good care," which is seen in His concern, His thoughts, and His willingness to do something about it. So who cares? God cares. He cares for you! In fact, He cares much more about you than you care about you. Take your bad cares from the past, the present, and the future and place them on God's good care. That is the only way to live a carefree life. Who cares? God cares.

MEDITATION 8

■ ■ ■

PRIDE GOES BEFORE WORRY AND A HAUGHTY SPIRIT BEFORE FEAR (PROUD PEOPLE SHOULD BE AFRAID).

This is what God says.

Job 15:24–25

Trouble and anguish shall make him afraid; they shall prevail against him, as a king ready to the battle. For he stretcheth out his hand against God, and strengtheneth himself against the Almighty.

Now think about it.

For the stubbornly proud individual, trouble, distress, anguish, and the hopelessness of being trapped and cornered by a powerful, relentless, enemy king (poised and ready to do battle) will make him afraid, fill him with terror, and make him realize that he is not as powerful as he thinks he is but could be overcome by someone stronger than he; those he is afraid of will prevail against him and overpower him. This proud individual should be afraid because he proudly stretched out his hand and shook his fist at God, and arrogantly defied the almighty God.

How can this affect me?

Proud people pretend that they have it all together and that nothing really scares them. Proud people pretend to be in control when they should be genuinely afraid. Solomon wisely warns us that "pride goeth before destruction and a haughty spirit before a fall" (Proverbs 16:18). Pride is nothing more than a big, fat liar. Arrogance is one of the greatest deceivers alive today. When you think more highly of yourself than you should, you will soon be brought down (and the fall could be quite painful and embarrassing). Are you bigger than your God? Do you complain and proudly disagree with what He is doing in your life? Are you angry with God? Do you (in your own subtle way) shake your fist in disgust with something that God has done? When you take life into your own hands and push God aside, you had better fear. When you refuse to see anyone's side of things (even God's) other than your own, you should be afraid. Do you struggle with thinking that you are better than others? Are your time, your comfort, your desires, your wants, all that are important to you? When you go after God Almighty, when you shake your head in disgust and your fist in defiance against Him, you can look forward to one thing: trouble, distress, anguish, and hopelessness. Proud people should be genuinely afraid.

This is what God says.

Proverbs 16:18

Pride goeth before destruction, and an haughty spirit before a fall.

Now think about it.

Pride, selfishness, and arrogant self-confidence set you up for destruction, and a haughty spirit, a no-one-can-tell-me-I'm-wrong attitude is in control of your thinking just before you fall into sin.

How does this affect me?

What is your attitude toward the habitual sin of worry? What do you think about the sin of faithlessness? If you proudly think you not only know when to stop worrying but can stop anytime you choose, you're fooling yourself. If you've got the attitude that you can continue in your sinful worry without experiencing any negative consequences, you're fooling yourself. If you refuse pastoral counsel and ignore basic Bible teaching with the no-one-can-tell-me-I'm-wrong attitude because I have a right and a reason to fear and worry, get ready for disappointment and destruction. Your hope will be destroyed. Your relationships will be destroyed. Your confidence will be destroyed. Your walk with God will be destroyed. Those who life themselves high above God's clear warnings will fall so fast and so far that they hardly ever crawl out of their destruction. Worry leads to worry. Fear leads to fear. If you proudly ignore those who are trying to help you, if you haughtily despise the counsel and encouragement from friends, if you think you are big enough to handle these issues in your own strength, get read to fall. Before destruction the heart of man is haughty, and before honor is humility (Proverbs

18:12). A proud heart makes you think you can do it. You can fight this thing off. You can find total victory in yourself. You have the strength to be in control over your fear and worry. You can win! A humble heart realizes you can't do it. Left to yourself you will be defeated. You alone will be under the control and domination of your faithlessness, worry, and anxiety. You will lose the battle if you don't get help.

MEDITATION 9

■ ■ ■

I CAN'T BUT GOD CAN.

This is what God says.

Deuteronomy 20:1–4

When thou goest out to battle against thine enemies, and seest horses, and chariots, and a people more than thou, be not afraid of them: for the Lord thy God is with thee, which brought thee up out of the land of Egypt. And it shall be, when ye are come nigh unto the battle, that the priest shall approach and speak unto the people, and shall say unto them, Hear, O Israel, ye approach this day unto battle against your enemies: let not your hearts faint, fear not, and do not tremble, neither be ye terrified because of them; for the Lord your God is he that goeth with you, to fight for you against your enemies, to save you.

Now think about it.

When you go out to battle against your enemies and you see their powerful horses, swift and sophisticated chariots, and a huge army of soldiers (much larger than your own), don't allow fear to consume your heart; don't be afraid of them; always remember that the omnipotent, almighty Lord your God is with you, the same God that protected your ancestors with a fiery cloud and destroyed the Egyptian army in the Red Sea when He brought your people out of the land of Egypt. When you are approaching the battlefield and are on the verge of fighting your enemy, the priest will remind your army and encourage them by saying, "Israel, listen closely. Today you will meet your enemies in battle, do not be fainthearted (the Lord is with you), do not fear (the Lord is with you), do not tremble (the Lord is with you), do not be terrified because of your enemies for the Lord your God is going with you, He will fight your enemies for you, and He will save you.

How can this affect me?

When you come face to face with insurmountable odds, unreasonable conflicts, and irreducible obstacles, what do you do? What do you think? How do you approach a situation (that humanly speaking) is impossible? How can you boldly stand with confidence as you look such fear in the face? If you trust in your own strength, you can't! If you are confident in your own abilities, the situation remains impossible. When you say, "I can do all things!" and leave off the phrase "through Christ who strengthens me," you will soon realize that you can do nothing. Once you understand and know deep within your soul that you cannot deal with the seeming impossible, you are ready to trust a God Who can! Forcing yourself to turn your focus off your fears and frailties enables you to focus on a Father Who fears nothing and no one. No matter how big the enemy, God is bigger. No matter how strong the foe, God is stronger. No matter how impossible the situation, God is the God of the impossible. You can't, but God can.

> ■ ■ ■
>
> REMEMBER,
> YOU CAN'T,
> BUT GOD CAN.
>
> ■ ■ ■

Israel's spiritual leaders faced a seemingly indestructible army by encouraging Israel, saying, "Israel, listen closely. Today you will meet your enemies in battle, do not be fainthearted (the Lord is with you), do not fear (the Lord is with you), do not tremble (the Lord is with you), do not be terrified because of your enemies, for the Lord your God is going with you, He will fight your enemies for you, He will save you."

Paul encouraged the Philippian Christians by saying, "I can do all things through Christ, Who constantly is strengthening me."

Jesus helped the apostles change their focus by saying, "With men it is impossible, but not with God: for with God all things are possible."

Paul comforted the young believers in Ephesus when he penned, "Now unto Him Who is able to do exceeding abundantly above all that we ask, think, or even imagine, according to His incredible power that works in us."

Jeremiah comforted his listeners as he wrote, "Ah, Lord God! You made the heaven and the earth by Your great, powerful, outstretched arm. There is nothing too hard for You. Nothing!"

Remember, you can't, but God can. Take the advice written down for you from Moses, Jeremiah, Paul, and Jesus Himself: God is the God of the impossible.

This is what God says.

Matthew 14:25–27

And in the fourth watch of the night Jesus went unto them, walking on the sea. And when the disciples saw him walking on the sea, they were troubled, saying, It is a spirit; and they cried out for fear. But straightway Jesus spake unto them, saying, Be of good cheer; it is I; be not afraid.

Now think about it.

And in the fourth watch of the night (just before dawn between 3:00 and 6:00) Jesus went to them, miraculously walking on the Sea of Galilee. And when the disciples saw Him walking on the sea (knowing that they were by now three or four miles from shore), they were terrified, troubled, and cried out in fear saying, "It's a ghost!" But immediately Jesus said to them, "Don't be afraid, cheer up, and take courage; it is not a ghost, but it is I, Jesus."

How can this affect me?

Sometimes we wonder why the Lord does not seem to come to rescue us until the "fourth watch of the night." By the "fourth watch" we are well wearied and overwrought as we have struggled through the first three watches. It seems when our strength is totally depleted, our Lord comes. When we know we cannot save ourselves, our Lord comes. When we are about to lose all hope, the Lord comes. When the storm seems unbearable and rescue impossible, the Lord comes. Lazarus lay dead in the grave for several days before the Lord came. Jesus could have prevented Lazarus's death or healed him from a distance, but by His waiting Lazarus experienced the life-changing power of God and Mary and Martha viewed the almighty glory of God. Our fretting and worrying during the first, second, and third watches reveal a puny faith in a powerful God. Our complaining and discontent give evidence that we do not know or trust our God very well. The twelve apostles, hands tightly grasping the oars and arms wearied from rowing, could not bring the ship to shore without some kind of miraculous intervention from God. Jesus was not late in coming but, in His sovereignty, right on time. Until our desperation turns to dependence and our terror turns to trust, we will probably continue to paddle hard only to remain in the middle of our storm far from the security of the shore. Do not fear during the first watch. Refuse to live in terror through the second watch. Don't lose hope or heart in the third watch. In the fourth watch of the night, the God Who can subdue even the laws of nature will come walking to you. If you expect Him to come, you will rejoice with relief. If you doubt His coming, His ghostlike presence may scare you too. Cheer up! Take heart! Take courage! Don't be afraid . . . dawn is just ahead.

MEDITATION 10

■ ■ ■

THE MORE WE SIN,
THE MORE WE FEAR.

This is what God says.

Joshua 8:1

And the Lord said unto Joshua, Fear not, neither be thou dismayed: take all the people of war with thee, and arise, go up to Ai: see, I have given into thy hand the king of Ai, and his people, and his city, and his land.

Now think about it.

The Lord said to Joshua, "Fear not. Don't be dismayed or discouraged but take your entire army and attack your enemy Ai. You will see the victory I will give you. You will defeat the powerful king of Ai and his armies. You will capture his city and his land."

How can this affect me?

Why did Joshua fear? Why was Joshua so discouraged? Why did Joshua lack the confidence to face his enemy after what he saw God do to the wicked people of Jericho? Why? Because his last attempt had ended in defeat. Even though the enemy were not that big, they were too big for Joshua. He failed. He was beaten down. Thirty-six men died while the rest of his men cowardly turned and ran away from the seemingly tiny foe. Why? Why the defeat? Why the fear? Why the cowardice? Why the lack of confidence? Sin. Sin is a professional thief that robs us of all our confidence. You cannot live in sin and trust God at the same time. Sin subtly creeps into our hearts and robs us of our dependence on God, turning us into fearful cowards. The more we sin, the more we fear. The more we sin, the more we fall. The more frequently we sin, the more easily we get discouraged. To renew our confidence, we must repent of our sin. Admit it, confess it, and forsake it.

Even though Joshua did not know about Achan's greed, he was operating on a false confidence as he sent men to attack Ai. He had done it before and knew he could do it again. He forgot to seek God's will in the battle. If he had gone to God before he went to Ai, God would have told him not to go until the sin was dealt with. We can easily fall into the same trap as we habitually race through our lives doing what we think is

right without daily seeking God's will. As Joshua saw the young wives and fatherless children of the thirty-six men that died in battle, his heart must have been overcome with regrets as he thought, "I wish I had sought God's face about this. I am so sorry, Lord. I know You have forgiven me, but I cannot change the consequences of my actions." If you want to eliminate fear and discouragement from your life, start each morning seeking God's will through His Word. Daily ask God for the wisdom He promises to give. Go to God before you go to battle. Do not face your enemies until you have been with your Lord. "Fear not and don't be dismayed."

This is what God says.

Romans 13:1–4

Let every soul be subject unto the higher powers. For there is no power but of God: the powers that be are ordained of God. Whosoever therefore resisteth the power, resisteth the ordinance of God: and they that resist shall receive to themselves damnation. For rulers are not a terror to good works, but to the evil. Wilt thou then not be afraid of the power? do that which is good, and thou shalt have praise of the same: for he is the minister of God to thee for good. But if thou do that which is evil, be afraid; for he beareth not the sword in vain: for he is the minister of God, a revenger to execute wrath upon him that doeth evil.

Now think about it.

Let every one of us be subject (submissive and obedient) unto all governing authorities (powers) in our lives. There is no authority except from God. All known authorities that exist today are appointed, ordained, and established by God (this includes government leaders, police, employers, bosses, managers, principals, teachers, pastors, moms, and dads). Therefore, whoever rebels against (resists) authority rebels against God by opposing the ordinance of God. They that resist will receive condemnation on themselves (God will judge in His way and in His time). You do not have to fear any authority if you do that which is good, but if you do evil by resisting their commands, you will fear. Do you want to be unafraid of the authorities in your life? Then simply do what is right! Not only will you not fear, but your authorities will praise and honor you for doing right. Whether you know it or not, all authorities are servants of God established for your protection and your good. But if you do that which is evil, you had better be afraid, for authorities do not bear the sword for nothing (they have the power and authority to punish sin, rebellion, and disobedience). Remember, they are the servants of God, sent for the purpose of punishing those who do evil.

How can this affect me?

Do you want to be unafraid of the authorities? Then do what is right.

Do you want to be unafraid of your boss? Then work hard and don't be lazy.

Do you want to be unafraid of getting points on your record and a $125 fine? Then don't speed.

Do you want to be unafraid of being grounded for life? Then don't sneak out of the house against your parents' permission.

Do you want to be unafraid of an income tax audit? Then be honest and don't cheat on your taxes.

Do you want to be unafraid of getting caught looking on someone else's paper in class? Then study hard before the test and don't cheat.

Do you want to be unafraid of getting caught viewing inappropriate material on the Internet? Then get a filter and don't click on the wicked sites.

Do you want to be unafraid of getting restrictions on your cell phone or car? Then be wise in the way you use both of them.

Do you want to be unafraid of getting drunk and inadvertently committing vehicular manslaughter? Then don't drink alcoholic beverages.

Do you want to be unafraid of getting kicked out of your school? Then don't break the rules.

Do you want to be unafraid of getting fired from work? Then work hard and go the extra mile to make your employer successful.

Do you want to be unafraid of suffering the consequences of your sin by spending eternity in hell? Then humble yourself before God, admit your sin, seek God's forgiveness, and trust Christ alone for your salvation.

Do you want to be unafraid of the authorities? Then do what is right!

Part**Two**

GOD'S WORD APPLIED TO TEN COMMON FEARS

What does God say about

- the fear of death?

- the fear of being alone?

- the fear of the future?

- the fear of failure?

- the fear of rejection?

- the fear of financial problems?

- the fear of people?

- the fear of public speaking?

- the fear of relationships?

- the fear of wasting my life?

FEAR 1

■ ■ ■

THE FEAR OF DEATH VS. THE FACT OF GOD'S SOVEREIGNTY

(THE FEAR OF FLYING, HEIGHTS, SPIDERS, CANCER, STORMS, AND OTHER DEATH-THREATENING EXPERIENCES)

This is what God says.

Psalm 27:3–5

Though an host should encamp against me, my heart shall not fear: though war should rise against me, in this will I be confident. One thing have I desired of the Lord, that will I seek after; that I may dwell in the house of the Lord all the days of my life, to behold the beauty of the Lord, and to inquire in his temple. For in the time of trouble he shall hide me in his pavilion: in the secret of his tabernacle shall he hide me; he shall set me up upon a rock.

Now think about it.

Even though an entire enemy army would set up camp and surround me, my heart will not fear! Even though this enemy's huge host of warriors would declare war and rise against me to destroy me, I will be confident! The same comforting truth that gives me confidence and courage against my enemies here on earth is the one thing I desire and have asked of the Lord and will long for. Here it is. I desire to dwell in the house of the Lord all the days of my eternal life. I desire to behold the beauty of the Lord and gaze at His glory forever. I desire to spend an eternity inquiring in God's presence to find out Who He is so that I can praise, honor, and love Him more. But until then I know He will take care of me. For in my times of trouble, fear, and difficulties, He will hide me in His pavilion and in the secret places of His tabernacle. He will set me upon a rock where I am safe and secure in His protection.

How can this affect me?

Do you fear death? David knew he had enemies but he did not know how or when they would attack. Some of his enemies were like starving vultures ready to attack suddenly, impulsively, and without notice. Other enemies were more like hired barbarians who were willing to settle down for a prolonged siege and wait for David to give up or to starve to death. The fear of death works the same way. Some of us will die from a prolonged illness such as cancer or Alzheimer's, while others will die quickly from a tragic accident or a heart attack. Either way, the enemy of death will encamp its armies around you. Do you fear death? Death is inevitable. We all have a set appointment on God's calendar with death. "It is appointed unto man once to die" (Hebrews 9:27). David left his father's sheep to serve King Saul both in his courts and on his battlefields, facing death every day. How can anyone live while staring death in the face day after day? The only way is to follow David's example and look past the ugly face of death right into the beauty of God presence. To be absent from the body is to be in the presence of the Lord. David stood on a high rock looking at his vast enemy encamped against him and said, "My heart will not fear! I am confident of what will happen after death. What my enemy thinks will be a victory for him will actually be a victory for me! I will die and be ushered into the very presence of God. My heart will not fear!" David was ready to trade the discomfort of hiding in caves and forests with the joy of dwelling in God's house. David was eager to leave the presence of his hateful enemies, his troubles, and his heartaches to abide in the presence of his loving Lord. David couldn't wait to remove from his eyes the ugliness of war-maddened, blood-soaked barbarians and fix them on the beauty of the holiness, righteousness, and love of a glorious God. David refused to fear death but rather welcomed it as the narrow passageway from troubles, hurt, and fear to love, joy, and peace. David refused to fear death. Do you fear death?

This is what God says.

Matthew 10:28–31

And fear not them which kill the body, but are not able to kill the soul: but rather fear him which is able to destroy both soul and body in hell. Are not two sparrows sold for a farthing? and one of them shall not fall on the ground without your Father. But the very hairs of your head are all numbered. Fear ye not therefore, ye are of more value than many sparrows.

Now think about it.

Believer, do not be terrified, frightened, and fearful of those who can only kill your body (which for believers will be resurrected again someday) but are not able to kill your soul (not even Satan can touch your eternal soul): but rather fear, respect, and give reverential awe to God, Who is able to destroy both soul and body in hell and has the power over the eternal existence of all men. (Be in fearful awe of a God Who truly loves you and cares for you.) Are not two, tiny sparrows sold for what would be pennies today? Even though they seem worthless to some, a little sparrow cannot fall to the ground without God (your heavenly Father) knowing and caring. God knows all about you . . . even the number of hairs on your head . . . and He cares for you. Knowing that you have a God Who knows what is going on in your life and cares for you, don't be afraid of any enemy that seeks to destroy you. Remember, you are more valuable to God than many sparrows.

How can this affect me?

Did you know that you are important to God? God sees value and worth in a tiny sparrow. Sparrows are too small to carry burdens, too flighty to work, too minute to awe or inspire with their strength of flight, too dependent to depend on. Sparrows need God to survive and in their own way trust Him. No matter how small, weak, insignificant, or unimportant you may view yourself, you are important to God. Do you fear death? Is it death itself or the process of death that you fear? Is it fear of the unknown? Fear of the pain? Fear of being forgotten? Fear that you may not go to heaven? Death is the wage, the earnings, the take-home pay for all whose sin has not been confessed and forgiven. Death, at least for a while, is separation from those you love. Eternal death is eternal separation from God and those who have trusted God to save their eternal souls. Those who have trusted Christ for eternal life need never to fear eternal death. Knowing this, why do we still fear death? We sometimes forget that God does care. In God's sight, the death of believers is a precious thing because He then has those believers in His presence, where He can protect and provide for them.

Many who fear death wrestle with the belief that God values them like they value themselves. Seldom do we value ourselves in the same way God does. While some struggle with the prideful, selfish, paralyzing mindset of what some call a low self-image (verbalizing their supposed lack of looks, talents, or purpose), others humbly view themselves only as weak, inconsistent, undeserving sinners to whom the reality of forgiveness is an ever-illusive truth. Both approaches to self appraisal will lead to unhealthy, unbiblical thinking. Those who seek glory and attempt to gain attention by spouting their low self-image to everyone they meet are actually praise mongers, baiting their listeners to respond in admiration and adoration, thus feeding

■■■

YOU ARE IMPORTANT TO GOD.

■■■

their selfishness and pride all the more. Those who paint their self portrait with brush strokes of defeat, failure, and unworthiness may be honest in their appraisal but are forgetting that when God paints a portrait of those who are "in Christ," you will see nothing but Christ on the canvas. When God looks at those of us who are in Christ, He does not focus on our sinfulness but on Christ's righteousness; He does not see our wickedness but Christ's holiness; He does not gaze on our foolishness but on Christ's wisdom. Remember, God sees value and worth in a tiny sparrow. No matter how small, weak, insignificant, or unimportant you may view yourself, you are important to God.

How do I know that God is sovereign?

With each passage below, read what God says, think about it, and meditate on how His sovereignty personally affects you.

Job 11:7–9

Canst thou by searching find out God? canst thou find out the Almighty unto perfection? It is as high as heaven; what canst thou do? deeper than hell; what canst thou know? The measure thereof is longer than the earth, and broader than the sea.

Isaiah 46:8–10

Remember this, and shew yourselves men: bring it again to mind, O ye transgressors. Remember the former things of old: for I am God, and there is none else; I am God, and there is none like me, declaring the end from the beginning, and from ancient times the things that are not yet done, saying, My counsel shall stand, and I will do all my pleasure.

Psalm 33:8–11

Let all the earth fear the Lord: let all the inhabitants of the world stand in awe of him. For he spake, and it was done; he commanded, and it stood fast. The Lord bringeth the counsel of the heathen to nought: he maketh the devices of the people of none effect. The counsel of the Lord standeth for ever, the thoughts of his heart to all generations.

FEAR 2

■ ■ ■

THE FEAR OF BEING ALONE VS. THE FACT OF GOD'S OMNIPRESENCE

(THE FEAR OF LONELINESS, DEATH OF A LOVED ONE, SINGLENESS, ETC.)

This is what God says.

John 14:26–27

But the Comforter, which is the Holy Ghost, whom the Father will send in my name, he shall teach you all things, and bring all things to your remembrance, whatsoever I have said unto you. Peace I leave with you, my peace I give unto you: not as the world giveth, give I unto you. Let not your heart be troubled, neither let it be afraid.

Now think about it.

In His farewell words to His twelve disciples, Jesus encouraged them by saying, "In My name, My Father will send to you His Holy Spirit, Who will be a Comforter and a Helper to you. The Holy Spirit will teach you all things and bring all things (everything I have already shown you and taught you) to your remembrance. (Just because I will not physically be with you, you will not forget everything you have learned.) Peace I leave with you and My peace I give to you. I do not give the kind of peace the world gives. Do not let your heart continue to be troubled. Don't be continually fearful. Don't be afraid."

How can this affect me?

There is a fear of losing those you love. There is a fear of never again seeing the ones you have grown to love the most. Life throws many such opportunities our way: military, college, marriage, job opportunities, war, rebellion, drugs, divorce, sickness, and even death. The ties of love are incredibly strong and the thought of not being with your family or friends can be devastating. In Scripture, men like Peter, Thomas, and Judas (not Iscariot) vocally struggled with the idea of Jesus leaving them. They loved Christ. They loved being with Christ. They may have thought that life could never be the same without being with Him. Jesus understood their fears and troubled hearts and sought to comfort them by promising the indwelling Holy Spirit. These guys needed faith to overcome their fear. They had to believe Christ's promise of His indwelling Spirit that would comfort their hearts to the point they could experience love, joy, and peace without Him physically being by their sides. God's Holy Spirit is a Comforter. He is a Helper. In a way that cannot be explained with words, God's Spirit reaches into a believer's troubled heart and overwhelms it with hope. Fear is a form of "no hope" thinking. Man's fear says, "I'll never be happy again. It will never be like it used to be. Life is not worth living. I can't handle this! Lord, why are You doing this to me?" God's peace says, "I want God's will, no matter how hard it may seem at times. I am thankful for God's comforting presence when there seems to be no one else around. God will get me through this! I know it will never be as bad as I am imagining it to be. Thank You, Lord, for everything You bring into my life. You do what is best for eternity for Your glory and the good of others." The peace that God gives will overcome the fear that we grasp.

This is what God says.

Lamentations 3:55–57

I called upon thy name, O Lord, out of the low dungeon. Thou hast heard my voice: hide not thine ear at my breathing, at my cry. Thou drewest near in the day that I called upon thee: thou saidst, Fear not.

Now think about it.

O Lord, from a dungeon, a deep pit, a place that I could never escape from in my own strength, I called on Your name. I know that You heard my voice. Please, Lord, do not hide Your ear from my sighing or ignore my cry for help. You were right there the day I called for You. You drew near to me and encouraged my heart by saying, "Don't fear. I am here!"

How can this affect me?

Have you ever been so deep in the pits that you wondered if anyone knew or even cared? Have you ever felt so enslaved by your worries and cares that there was literally no way out? Have you ever cried out for help only to wonder if your pleas ever left the room? If so, then you and the Old Testament prophet Jeremiah have a bit in common. God cares! God does hear our desperate cries for help and promises to "draw near" when we ask Him to. Living hundreds of years apart, Jeremiah and James both claimed this truth. James reminds us to "draw near to God and He will draw near to you." James may have read this prayerful plea from Jeremiah and knew that even though it was written hundreds of years before his time, God was still the same. Here we are, hundreds of years past James's time and guess what, God is still the same! The God of the Bible is the God of today. Our present-day dungeons may not be made of stone or rat infested, but they are as dark and dreary as a dungeon from any age or time. It is the promise of the presence of God that can open a window of light in such a dark prison. God will draw near when we ask Him and therefore, we can be as close to God as we want to be. In the pits? Enslaved by your problems? Hopelessly trapped? Draw near to God and you'll hear Him whisper, "Don't fear. I am here."

How do I know that God is omnipresent?

With each passage below, read what God says, think about it, and meditate on how His sovereignty personally affects you.

Matthew 28:20

Teaching them to observe all things whatsoever I have commanded you: and, lo, I am with you alway, even unto the end of the world. Amen.

Hebrews 13:5–6

Let your conversation be without covetousness; and be content with such things as ye have: for he hath said, I will never leave thee, nor forsake thee. So that we may boldly say, The Lord is my helper, and I will not fear what man shall do unto me.

Ephesians 3:16–17

That he would grant you, according to the riches of his glory, to be strengthened with might by his Spirit in the inner man; that Christ may dwell in your hearts by faith; that ye, being rooted and grounded in love.

FEAR 3

■ ■ ■

THE FEAR OF THE FUTURE VS. THE FACT OF GOD'S OMNISCIENCE

(THE FEAR OF THE UNKNOWN, JUDGMENT, FUTURE EVENTS, THE WHAT-IF WORLD, ETC.)

This is what God says.

1 Chronicles 22:11–13

Now, my son, the Lord be with thee; and prosper thou, and build the house of the Lord thy God, as he hath said of thee. Only the Lord give thee wisdom and understanding, and give thee charge concerning Israel, that thou mayest keep the law of the Lord thy God. Then shalt thou prosper, if thou takest heed to fulfil the statutes and judgments which the Lord charged Moses with concerning Israel: be strong, and of good courage; dread not, nor be dismayed.

Now think about it.

King David, speaking to his son Solomon said, "Now, my son, I pray that the Lord will be with you that you may prosper and be successful in building the house of the Lord your God, just as He has said you would. I know the Lord will give you discretion, wisdom, and understanding when He puts you in charge of Israel so that you may keep the law of the Lord your God. If you do everything you can to obey and fulfill the decrees, statutes, and judgments that the Lord gave Moses for Israel, you will prosper and be successful. Be strong. Be courageous. Do not be frightened or dread God's call for your life. Do not be scared, fearful, or dismayed."

How can this affect me?

Do you ever dread the future? Do you ever fear what God has called you or may call you to do? Do you lack the courage and strength to take that next step of faith in what God wants you to do? If so, step right along-side Solomon. Here is a young prince who had to follow in the footsteps of one of the greatest kings who ever lived. Here is a rising leader who was called upon to complete a task that would take multiple years, millions of dollars, and a massive amount of organizational skill to accomplish. Here is a dad who could encourage his son not because of the son's incredible abilities but because of God's power and promises. David knew that God wanted Solomon to build a temple even though Solomon doubted whether he could pull it off. David's confidence was served with a simple warning based on the conditional statement "Solomon, if you do everything you can to fulfill the statues and judgments the Lord gave you, you will be successful." Success, prosperity, accomplishments, achievements? IF! If you obey God's decrees, God will make you strong. If you fulfill God's judgments, God will give you courage. If you are careful to follow all God's commands, God will make you prosper. If you submit to God's statues, God will make you successful.

- If you—God will
- Don't dread the future
- If you—God will
- Don't fear what God has called you to do
- If you—God will

- You need not lack the courage and strength to take your next step
- If you—God will

Solomon built the temple. God did make him prosper. God did make him strong. God did give him wisdom. God will do the same for you. If you—God will.

This is what God says.

Isaiah 41:10–12

Fear thou not; for I am with thee: be not dismayed; for I am thy God: I will strengthen thee; yea, I will help thee; yea, I will uphold thee with the right hand of my righteousness. Behold, all they that were incensed against thee shall be ashamed and confounded: they shall be as nothing; and they that strive with thee shall perish. Thou shalt seek them, and shalt not find them, even them that contended with thee: they that war against thee shall be as nothing, and as a thing of nought.

Now think about it.

God says, "Fear not. You have no need to fear because I am with you. Do not allow yourself to be dismayed, discouraged, or downcast as you intently stare at the difficult situations you face, for I am your God (which, don't forget, means that you are My child). When you begin to fear the impossibilities of life, I will strengthen you by putting courage into your heart. I promise. Yes, I will help you by supporting you when you feel you are all alone and no one else cares. I promise. I will uphold you by grabbing hold of your hand with Mine (and with your hand in Mine I will help you do what is right). I promise. I want you to know that all those who burned in their anger against you will someday realize where they were wrong and be ashamed, disgraced, and even humiliated by the way they acted toward you. The day will come when it will seem like those who were so upset with you and caused such strife and contention never even existed. You won't be able to find them if you try. Those who made your life miserable will seemingly disappear. But I promise to be with you. When you need me, I'll always be available. When you cry out to me, I'll always listen. When you fear, I'll be there."

How can this affect me?

Fear, worry, discouragement, loneliness, and depression are often a result of a wrong focus. What we dwell on in our minds is what controls us (at least as long as we insist on dwelling on it). Worriers live in a "what if" world rather than a "what is" world.

- What if my friends really don't like me?
- What if I have cancer?
- What if I never get married?
- What if I lose my job?
- What if my child dies?
- What if I get Alzheimer's and can't take care of myself?
- What if I can't pay my bills?
- What if my husband finds another woman?
- What if my children hate me?
- What if?

The "WHAT-IF" world is a sad and depressing place to live. The sun never shines. Every day storm clouds hover over its downcast dwellers. In a way it's a scary place to live too. There are wild beasts that roam freely looking for some fearful man, woman, or child to devour. Death, Discouragement, Hatred, and Loneliness are the names of just a few of the run-down towns that dot its muddy roads. Neighbors rush out of their dreary cottages to do what is necessary to survive and race back in without caring for those who live on either side of them. Few smile. How can they? You see, the god of the "WHAT-IF" world is quite small. He is powerful, but not all-powerful. He is wise, but not all-wise. He is kind of in control, but not enough to handle the "what ifs" that inevitably will come. Every once in a while someone bolsters up the courage to pack his U-Haul and leave the "WHAT-IF" world for the "WHAT-IS" world.

The "WHAT-IS" world still has clouds, rain, and dark days. It has some of the same towns along its way, but few people choose to live there. It has its wild beasts and its uncaring neighbors. The difference is the smiles. Why? The God of the "WHAT-IS" world is amazing. He is not just powerful, but all-powerful, totally omnipotent, and greater than any other force in the entire universe (including death and discouragement). He is not just wise, but all-wise, amazingly omniscient, and knows what is best for our lives. He is not just a little in control, but sovereign, always in control and will accomplish His will in our lives. He is there for those who love Him. He is there for those who are struggling. He is there for those who are hurting. He is! Those who choose to live in the "WHAT-IS" world choose to live by faith in a God Who cares about every dark day. They believe in a God Who is! In fact, they know that without faith it is impossible to please God and when they come to God they believe that He is real, that He is powerful, that He is caring, that He is forgiving, that He is a rewarder of them who diligently seek Him. To live in a "WHAT-IS" world, you must believe that God is . . . He is all He says He is. What world do you live in?

How do I know that God is omniscient?

With each passage below, read what God says, think about it, and meditate on how His sovereignty personally affects you.

Psalm 139:1–6

O Lord, thou hast searched me, and known me. Thou knowest my downsitting and mine uprising, thou understandest my thought afar off. Thou compassest my path and my lying down, and art acquainted with all my ways. For there is not a word in my tongue, but, lo, O Lord, thou knowest it altogether. Thou hast beset me behind and before, and laid thine hand upon me. Such knowledge is too wonderful for me; it is high, I cannot attain unto it.

Proverbs 5:21

For the ways of man are before the eyes of the Lord, and he pondereth all his goings.

Romans 11:33–36

O the depth of the riches both of the wisdom and knowledge of God! how unsearchable are his judgments, and his ways past finding out! For who hath known the mind of the Lord? or who hath been his counselor? Or who hath first given to him, and it shall be recompensed unto him again? For of him, and through him, and to him, are all things: to whom be glory for ever. Amen.

Fear 4

■ ■ ■

The fear of failure vs. the fact of God's omnipotence

(The fear of failure, giving in to temptation, not making it on my own, failing in school, displeasing parents, etc.)

This is what God says.

Joshua 1:7–9

Only be thou strong and very courageous, that thou mayest observe to do according to all the law, which Moses my servant commanded thee: turn not from it to the right hand or to the left, that thou mayest prosper whithersoever thou goest. This book of the law shall not depart out of thy mouth; but thou shalt meditate therein day and night, that thou mayest observe to do according to all that is written therein: for then thou shalt make thy way prosperous, and then thou shalt have good success. Have not I commanded thee? Be strong and of a good courage; be not afraid, neither be thou dismayed: for the Lord thy God is with thee whithersoever thou goest.

Now think about it.

Joshua, be strong and very courageous that you may be careful to do everything that is in the law, which My servant Moses commanded you. Do not turn from it to the right nor to the left and you will prosper and be successful wherever you go. Do not let this book of the law (these writings of Mine; these very words that I give you) depart out of your mouth, be removed from your heart, or leave your mind. You must meditate on My words of comfort, guidance, and protection day and night, morning and evening. Then, every time you get a chance you will be careful to do everything that is written in it. Then you will be prosperous and successful. Have not I commanded you? Be strong and courageous! Do not tremble. Do not be afraid! Do not be dismayed! Why? For I, the Lord your God, will be with you wherever you go.

How can this affect me?

Joshua knew fear (but was successful in spite of his fears). A quick read through the book bearing his name will reveal the continuous thought "Be strong. Be courageous. Do not be afraid!" Joshua knew fear and God knew that Joshua knew fear. Over and over

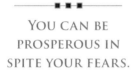

YOU CAN BE PROSPEROUS IN SPITE YOUR FEARS.

God encouraged and challenged him to get his focus off fear and on God. Why was Joshua so fearful? Why did he struggle so with fear? Did he fear defeat? Was he afraid he would fail God? Was it because he feared filling the shoes of the mighty Moses (a man who actually glowed after being in the very presence of God)? Was it because he was responsible for millions of rebellious, hardhearted, and unthankful people? Was it because he faced powerful giants that could potentially wipe out God's people in a single battle? Was it because he feared death? For Joshua, was it A, B, C, or all the above? Joshua had many factors on his plate that would have made most men or women give up in fear. How do your fears compare with Joshua's fears? Does your fear involve millions of people? Are there giants waiting to kill you? Are you afraid of failing? Defeat? Death? God offers to us the same encouragement He gave to Joshua . . . His presence. God promises to dwell in us, to stay with us, to never leave us, to never forsake us. His continual presence is demonstrated by His written Word. As you read and meditate on God's written words, you are acknowledging His presence. God spoke audibly to Moses and Joshua but wrote to us. Knowing how quickly we forget, God wrote a book! God has written down all He wants us to know. Joshua called it the "book of the law"; we call it the "Bible." The more you read and meditate on the omnipotence of God, the less you will fear God's inability to handle any situation. The more you read and meditate (day and night, by the way) on the omniscience of God, the less you will be afraid that God is clueless as to what is going on in your life. The more you read and meditate (morning and evening) on the omnipresence of God, the less you fear facing a terrifying experience without God being right by your side. Why fear when you can meditate on a God Who can make fear fear itself? Don't be afraid; be prosperous. Don't fear; be successful. Don't be dismayed; be strong in the Lord. You may know fear, but you can be prosperous (like Joshua) in spite of your fears.

This is what God says.

Psalm 55:22

Cast thy burden upon the Lord, and he shall sustain thee: he shall never suffer the righteous to be moved.

Now think about it.

Cast (totally let go so that God can totally control) your biggest burden and your most difficult trial on the Lord, and He will sustain you by never (never) permitting you (the righteous in Christ) to be moved, to be shaken, or to be made to fall.

How can this affect me?

There are those who attach their burdens to boomerangs. They want to give God a chance to deal with their difficulties but can't totally let go and trust God. There are others who put their burdens of life on a leash. They would rather not be burdened with such a heavy weight on their backs, but they must keep them within sight just in case God needs a little help. Some use the yo-yo approach to their heartaches by sending them God's way but quickly jerking them back into their own hands. You cannot "cast" and "hang-on" at the same time. You must let go! When God inspired David to write the word *cast*, He put the word in a tense that emphasizes the action itself but not the result of the action. In other words, we are to "cast" and any result of that "casting" comes from God and not from us. Our part is simple—just cast! Get rid of! Let go of your burden and don't take it back. Release your trial with no strings attached. Cast or get rid of everything that hinders your walk with God and in a metaphorical way chains, fetters, or imprisons you from what you could or should be doing. The word *burden* itself comes from a root meaning "to give." God, in a way, has given us our burdens to strengthen us and to give us opportunity to give them back to Him by trusting, leaning, and relying on Him more.

Once we "cast our burdens," God then promises to "sustain" us by keeping us from being "moved." When God sustains us, He grasps us in His hands and holds us in such a way that nothing can take us away. Jesus testified of this truth when He said, "My Father, which gave them to me (speaking of all believers), is greater than all; and no man is able to pluck them out of my

Father's hand." If you let go of your burdens, God will not let go of you!

Have you attached your burdens to a boomerang? Do you put a leash on your trials? Have you tied your anxious worries and cares on the end of a yo-yo string? If you want to live in the security and safety of God's hands, you had better let go of your burdens, trials, and cares. Cast your burdens on the Lord. He commands you to.

How do I know that God is omnipotent?

With each passage below, read what God says, think about it, and meditate on how His sovereignty personally affects you.

Psalm 91:1–7

He that dwelleth in the secret place of the most High shall abide under the shadow of the Almighty. I will say of the Lord, He is my refuge and my fortress: my God; in him will I trust. Surely he shall deliver thee from the snare of the fowler, and from the noisome pestilence. He shall cover thee with his feathers, and under his wings shalt thou trust: his truth shall be thy shield and buckler. Thou shalt not be afraid for the terror by night; nor for the arrow that flieth by day; nor for the pestilence that walketh in darkness;

nor for the destruction that wasteth at noonday. A thousand shall fall at thy side, and ten thousand at thy right hand; but it shall not come nigh thee.

Ephesians 1:19–23

And what is the exceeding greatness of his power to us-ward who believe, according to the working of his mighty power, which he wrought in Christ, when he raised him from the dead, and set him at his own right hand in the heavenly places, Far above all principality, and power, and might, and dominion, and every name that is named, not only in this world, but also in that which is to come: and hath put all things under his feet, and gave him to be the head over all things to the church, which is his body, the fulness of him that filleth all in all.

Revelation 1:8

I am Alpha and Omega, the beginning and the ending, saith the Lord, which is, and which was, and which is to come, the Almighty.

Fear 5

■ ■ ■

The fear of rejection vs. the fact of God's acceptance

(The fear of losing someone I love, divorce, having no friends, living my life all alone, never being liked, etc.)

This is what God says.

Isaiah 41:13

For I the Lord thy God will hold thy right hand, saying unto thee, Fear not; I will help thee.

Now think about it.

For I am the Lord your God. I will strengthen you, encourage you, stay with you by holding your right hand, saying unto you, "Fear not; I will help you."

How can this affect me?

When you were a little child, do you remember the difference between walking through a frighteningly dark room all alone and walking through the same room holding your dad's hand? Your dad's hand did not give the room more light, make it any safer, or free it from any monsters . . . but you did not have to worry about the darkness, dangers, or two-headed monsters with your hand tightly engulfed in your dad's hand. It is amazing how trust in someone or something bigger than yourself chases away fear. A dad is a dad but God is God! What type of "monster" do you fear in your adult life that is bigger or stronger than your God? With the Lord's help, three Hebrew young men walked in a fiery furnace, an old prophet walked around a lion's den, and Peter walked on water. A dad's hand can not only keep you from fear, it can keep you from falling. How many times would that preschool child skin his knee if dad did not have hold of his hand? How many times would that first grader trip over a rock, a curb, or a step if he did not tightly grip his father's hand? Dads are dads but God is God. God is the only one that can keep me from falling. As I continue to trust in Him, He will order my steps by His Word and not allow any sin, iniquity, or wickedness have dominion over me. God loves me, leads me, and lifts me up when I fall. I can trust my precious Lord's promise to Isaiah, "For I am the Lord your God. I will strengthen you, encourage you, stay with you by holding your right hand, saying unto you, 'Fear not; I will help you.'"

This is what God says.

Isaiah 43:1

But now thus saith the Lord that created thee, O Jacob, and he that formed thee, O Israel, Fear not: for I have redeemed thee, I have called thee by thy name; thou art mine.

Now think about it.

For so long, Jacob and Israel, you have been blind to what the Lord wanted to do for you, but now this is what the Lord has to say (remember Jacob, the Lord Who created you; and Israel, the Lord Who formed you), "Fear not, for I have redeemed you."

"Fear not, for I have called you by your name."

"Fear not, you are Mine."

How can this affect me?

There is something very special about family. I remember so vividly my ninety-six-year-old grandmother's response to me as I visited her in a nursing home. Her strength of mind had not kept up with her strength of body, and we could no longer look forward to her recognition of family members. I was quite close to this grandmother, for as a child I lived three years with her after sin destroyed my family. She sat staring into space aware of no one or nothing around her. As I knelt and tried to look into those distant eyes, a sparkle of recognition energized her whole body as she began to lift her shaking hand and spoke the words, "You are my people!" As her eyes were filled with recognition, mine were filled with tears. "You are my people!" I was hers. We were family. Close family. We had walked and talked and played and laughed together. Yes, I was her people and proud of it. I was her people and would do anything to please her. She remembered me. She cared.

> FEAR NOT,
> FOR I HAVE
> REDEEMED
> YOU.

How often does our Lord want us to respond to His words of ownership when we are paralyzed by fear, worry, and hurt? He wants us to seek His face and not allow the difficulties to consume our hearts. God is simply saying,

- Don't be afraid. You are Mine!
- Don't be afraid. I made you. You are Mine!
- Don't be afraid. I created you. You are Mine!
- Don't be afraid. I redeemed you. You are Mine!
- Don't be afraid. I know you. You are Mine!
- Don't be afraid. I love you. You are Mine!
- Don't be afraid. You are Mine!

How do I know that God accepts me?

With each passage below, read what God says, think about it, and meditate on how His sovereignty personally affects you.

Deuteronomy 31:6

Be strong and of a good courage, fear not, nor be afraid of them: for the Lord thy God, he it is that doth go with thee; he will not fail thee, nor forsake thee.

1 Samuel 12:2

For the Lord will not forsake his people for his great name's sake: because it hath pleased the Lord to make you his people.

Matthew 11:28–30

Come unto me, all ye that labour and are heavy laden, and I will give you rest. Take my yoke upon you, and learn of me; for I am meek and lowly in heart: and ye shall find rest unto your souls. For my yoke is easy, and my burden is light.

FEAR 6

■ ■ ■

THE FEAR OF FINANCIAL PROBLEMS VS. THE FACT OF GOD'S PROVISION

(THE FEAR OF FINANCIAL FAILURE, BANKRUPTCY, POVERTY, LOSING YOUR HOME, BEING FINANCIALLY DEPENDENT ON FAMILY, RETIREMENT SECURITY, RECESSION, ETC.)

This is what God says.

Philippians 4:19
But my God shall supply all your need according to his riches in glory by Christ Jesus.

Now think about it.

But my God will supply (He will fill full to overflowing) all your needs (every single one of them) according to His riches in glory in Christ Jesus (which include His influence, His presence, His compassion, His possessions, and His almighty power).

How can this affect me?

There is an economic principle called "supply and demand," which controls the prices and the availability of certain goods. The lower the supply and the higher the demand, the higher the cost and the lower the availability. I am thankful that God's ability to supply is never driven by anyone's demand. His resources are inexhaustible in His Son Christ Jesus. And speaking of demand, God is not saying that He will supply our demands (which are want-based rather than need-based) but our "needs." He knows what we have need of even before we ask Him. Some of our financial fears are not motivated by whether God is able to supply the need but by misunderstanding of the difference between wants and needs. What I want is not always what I need. What I need is not always what I want. The constant war between covetousness and contentment fuels this misunderstanding. Paul said that having something to eat and clothes to wear are all that we really need (1 Timothy 6:8). Jesus Himself said, "The foxes have holes, and the birds of the air have nests; but the Son of man hath not where to lay his head" (Matthew 8:20). Before we allow fear to grip our heart about a certain "need," we must look through the eyes of Scripture to discern whether it is a true need or a mere want. Most of our wants can be characterized by words such as *temporal, physical*, or *extravagant*. Needs, on the other hand, are usually associated with words such as *eternal*, *spiritual*, or *sufficient*. Once you determine that you have a real need, you can trust God to supply it in such a way that it will be more than you need. The Corinthian Christians heard this truth in these words, "And God is able to make all grace abound toward you; that ye, always having all sufficiency in all things, may abound to every good work" (2 Corinthians 9:8). Timothy said it well as he warned of covetousness (which has a direct link to wants) and pled for contentment (which is need-based). "But godliness with contentment is great gain." (The greatest gain you can achieve is not monetary, but godliness mixed with contentment will result in great gain.) "For we brought nothing into this world, and it is certain we can carry nothing out. [As helpless infants, we brought nothing into this world, and when we die we will take nothing

> **MOST OF OUR WANTS CAN BE CHARACTERIZED AS TEMPORAL.**

out of this world.] And having food [something to eat] and raiment [something to wear] let us be therewith content. But they that will be rich fall into temptation and a snare, and into many foolish and hurtful lusts, which drown men in destruction and perdition. [Those who desire to be rich and set their wills to be rich will fall into temptations, will get caught in devastating get-rich schemes, and will fall into many foolish, senseless, and harmful lusts that plunge people into an ocean of ruin and destruction where they will drown.] For the love of money is the root of all [kinds of] evil: which while some coveted after [some intensely craved for], they have erred [or wandered] from the faith [and what they once loved and believed], and pierced themselves through with many sorrows [the joy and happiness they thought the money would bring them was replaced by hurt and sorrow]" (1 Timothy 6:6–10).

This is what God says.

Proverbs 30:8–9

Remove far from me vanity and lies: give me neither poverty nor riches; feed me with food convenient for me: lest I be full, and deny thee, and say, Who is the Lord? or lest I be poor, and steal, and take the name of my God in vain.

Now think about it.

"Lord, remove far from me all empty thinking, foolishness, deceit, dishonesty, and lying. Give me neither poverty nor riches but feed me with the food that is needful for me and nothing more. If You give me too much and I am full, I may be tempted to forget about You and all Your goodness; think that I have gained all these riches in my own strength; and say, 'Who is the Lord?' If You give me too little to the extent of poverty, I may be tempted not to trust You, start stealing to meet my needs, and bring shame to Your holy name. I would hate for anyone to blaspheme You and take Your name in vain because it appeared that Your promise to supply everything I need looks like it is being broken."

How can this affect me?

We live in a world of extremes. Extreme sports. Extreme makeovers. Extreme extremes. When it comes to money problems, Solomon reminds us that we should steer clear of being extreme. We should not desire to be extremely rich and certainly do not want to be extremely poor. God wants us to be extremely satisfied with what He has already given us. A balanced view of money comes from a God-centered-life rather than a self-centered-life. Satisfaction in riches is supported by an eternal focus rather than a temporal focus. Too much and we are tempted to forget God. Too little and we are tempted to forsake God. In Deuteronomy 8, Moses explained this danger much better than I can.

Deuteronomy 8:11–18

Beware that thou forget not the Lord thy God, in not keeping his commandments, and his judgments, and his statutes, which I command thee this day: lest when thou hast eaten and art full, and hast built goodly houses, and dwelt therein; and when thy herds and thy flocks multiply, and thy silver and thy gold is multiplied, and all that thou hast is multiplied; then thine heart be lifted up, and thou forget the Lord thy God, which brought thee forth out of the land of Egypt, from the house of bondage; who led thee through that great and terrible wilderness, wherein were fiery serpents, and scorpions, and drought, where there was no water; who brought thee forth water out of the rock of flint; who fed thee in the wilderness with manna, which thy fathers knew not, that he might humble thee, and that he might prove thee, to do thee good at thy latter end; and thou say in thine heart, My power and the might of mine hand hath gotten me this wealth. But thou shalt remember the Lord thy God: for it is he that giveth thee power to get wealth that he may establish his covenant which he [promised] unto thy fathers, as it is this day."

It is so much better to be content than extreme. It is comforting to know that God has and will provide everything we need for our present happiness.

"Lord, thank you for giving me just enough. Not too much and not too little. I never want to forsake You or to forget You. Thank You for providing just what I need. I trust You Lord, and You alone."

How do I know that God will provide?

With each passage below, read what God says, think about it, and meditate on how His sovereignty personally affects you.

Psalm 23:1–6

The Lord is my shepherd; I shall not want. He maketh me to lie down in green pastures: he leadeth me beside the still waters. He restoreth my soul: he leadeth me in the paths of righteousness for his name's sake. Yea, though I walk through the valley of the shadow of death, I will fear no evil: for thou art with me; thy rod and thy staff they comfort me. Thou preparest a table before me in the presence of mine enemies: thou anointest my head with oil; my cup runneth over. Surely goodness and mercy shall follow me all the days of my life: and I will dwell in the house of the Lord for ever.

Psalm 84:11–12

For the Lord God is a sun and shield: the Lord will give grace and glory: no good thing will he withhold from them that walk uprightly. O Lord of hosts, blessed is the man that trusteth in thee.

Proverbs 3:9–10

Honour the Lord with thy substance, and with the firstfruits of all thine increase: so shall thy barns be filled with plenty, and thy presses shall burst out with new wine.

Fear 7

■ ■ ■

The fear of people vs. the fear of God

(The fear of peer pressure, being mocked or laughed at, being talked into sin, not being accepted, not pleasing others, etc.)

This is what God says.

1 Peter 3:13–16

And who is he that will harm you, if ye be followers of that which is good? But and if ye suffer for righteousness' sake, happy are ye: and be not afraid of their terror, neither be troubled; but sanctify the Lord God in your hearts: and be ready always to give an answer to every man that asketh you a reason of the hope that is in you with meekness and fear: having a good conscience; that, whereas they speak evil of you, as of evildoers, they may be ashamed that falsely accuse your good conversation in Christ.

Now think about it.

Who is there to harm and mistreat you if you zealously pursue what is good? And if you do suffer for righteousness' sake (for faithfully doing what is right), you will be blessed and happy. Just as Isaiah said, "Be not afraid of their terror [do not fear what they fear], neither be troubled [nor should you dread anyone but God. Our reverential fear and awe-inspired dread should never be toward mere men but reserved only for our almighty, all-powerful Lord God]." Instead, set apart (sanctify) Christ as Lord in your hearts and always be ready (perpetual, incessant readiness not hindered by laziness, weariness, or selfishness) to gently and kindly give an answer to everyone who asks you why you are so joyful, peaceful, and full of hope in our sad, troubled, and hopeless world! And keep a good conscience so that those who speak maliciously against you, and through gossip attack your good behavior in Christ by falsely accusing you of participating in evil, may be ashamed of their slander and embarrassed by their lies as they watch and observe your Christlike lifestyle.

How can this affect me?

Whom do you fear? Whom do you dread seeing at school, at church, or at work? Are you plagued by fear because of a bully in your life? Who is he that can harm you when Christ is the Lord of your life? Who seems bigger than God in your eyes? Who is keeping you from what God wants you to be? Who is it that causes you to forget that the Lord is on your side and you do not need to fear? What can any man do to you? Who causes you to doubt what David said, "In God have I put my trust. I will not be afraid what man can do unto me"? Who makes you forget the way God protected the three Hebrew children in the fiery furnace when the king cried, "Lo, I see four men loose, walking in the midst of the fire, and they have no hurt, and the form of the fourth is like the Son of God"?

How can we face spiritual bullies with confidence that God is on our side? How can we keep from forgetting God's promises to protect, provide, and strengthen us against verbal attacks from those who refuse to fear God? Under inspiration of the Holy Spirit of God, Peter gives us the answer to these questions. Peter himself had to learn from experience (a sad experience I am sure he wished had never taken place). Fear caused Peter to deny his Lord three times! Years later he penned the words we are meditating on today. God replaced his fear with courage and his apprehension with confidence. Here is Peter's experiential and inspired advice: make Christ Lord of your heart, know why you believe what you believe, and keep a good conscience by doing right in the sight of God.

Set apart Christ as Lord in your heart (sanctify the Lord God in your hearts).

> We sanctify the Lord God in our hearts when we with sincerity and fervency adore Him, when our thoughts of Him are awful and reverend, when we rely upon His power, trust His faithfulness, submit to His wisdom, imitate His holiness, and give Him the glory due to His most illustrious perfections. We sanctify God before others when our deportment is such as invites and encourages others to glorify and honor Him. (Matthew Henry, *Matthew Henry's Commentary*. 6 vols. [rev. 1706–1721, PC Study Bible Formatted Electronic Database, 2006 Biblesoft])

Be ready to give a reason for why you believe what you believe ("be ready always to give an answer to every man that asketh you a reason of the hope that is in you with meekness and fear").

Always be prepared to give a simple, biblical reason for why you do what you do! If you know "why" you live the way you do, when confronted, you can give a solid "defense" rather than become sadly defensive. Make sure your disposition matches your position. Be kind and honest. Be meek and strong. Be gentle and forceful.

> ■ ■ ■
>
> GIVE A SOLID "DEFENSE" RATHER THAN BECOME DEFENSIVE.
>
> ■ ■ ■

A proud, arrogant, know-it-all attitude will negate your entire defense or reason. A humble, gentle, "I-want-what-is-best-for-you" attitude at least gives your defense a chance of being listened to and responded to. Study the Word of God to know why you believe what you believe. Meditate on Scripture to know why you do what you do. Always be ready to give a good Bible answer to anyone who questions God, His Word, or your life.

Keep a good conscience ("having a good conscience; that, whereas they speak evil of you, as of evildoers, they may be ashamed that falsely accuse your good conversation in Christ").

It is a very terrible thing to let conscience begin to grow hard, for it soon chills into northern iron and steel. It is like the freezing of a pond. The first film of ice is scarcely perceptible; keep the water stirring and you will prevent the frost from hardening it. But once let it film over and remain quiet, the glaze thickens over the surface and it thickens still, and at last it is so firm that a wagon might be drawn over the solid ice. So with conscience, it films over gradually, until at last it becomes hard and unfeeling and is not crushed even with ponderous loads of iniquity. (Charles Haddon Spurgeon, *The Biblical Illustrator*, Old Testament vol. by Joseph Exell [1887, London. Electronic Database, 2002, 2003, 2006 Ages Software, Inc. and Biblesoft])

This is what God says.

Ezekiel 3:8–11

Behold, I have made thy face strong against their faces, and thy forehead strong against their foreheads. As an adamant harder than flint have I made thy forehead: fear them not, neither be dismayed at their looks, though they be a rebellious house. Moreover he said unto me, Son of man, all my words that I shall speak unto thee receive in thine heart, and hear with thine ears. And go, get thee to them of the captivity, unto the children of thy people, and speak unto them, and tell them, Thus saith the Lord God; whether they will hear, or whether they will forbear.

Now think about it.

I will never forget what God told me: "Ezekiel, I will enable you to stand face to face with these rebellious people. Whatever intimidating look they throw your way, you will be able to look straight in their eyes the very same way. I will make you as stubborn, unyielding, and hardheaded as they are (but not in a sinful way). I will give you absolute determination, which will be seen in your unstoppable resolve, purpose, fortitude, and grit; specifically your countenance (namely your forehead) will appear like a flint or a diamond, the hardest of stones, which can scratch or make a mark on the hardest of stones or metals but refuses to be marked by any of these same substances. Ezekiel, do not be afraid of these hardened rebels or terrified by these obstinate children (even though they are a rebellious group to deal with)." And then the Lord continued, "Ezekiel, you need to listen very carefully, understand, and take to heart every word I say to you. It is now time to go to your peers, your own countrymen who are in exile, and say to them, 'Listen to the Lord God! This is what the sovereign Lord says! Listen to Him!' By the way, Ezekiel, keep speaking to them whether or not they will listen to you."

How can this affect me?

Can fear affect your appearance? Do people in your life affect the way you look? What happens to you when the people in your life are big and the God in your life is small? Why is it that people can change your countenance but God can't? Your fear of others not only furrows your brow but also removes the sparkle in your eyes. Your obvious intimidation by those you hardly know changes a pleasing smile into a perpetual frown. When people oppose you, do you hold your head high with confidence or stare at the ground? When your family upsets you, do you respond with the assurance seen in a man of purpose or do you shuffle your feet as seen in a man of defeat? Do people scare you? Do stubborn, unyielding, hardheaded disagreeable people make you want to run and hide? Again, what happens to you when the people in your life are big and the God in your life is small? What God did for Ezekiel He can do for you! Do you believe God when He says,

"I will enable you to stand face to face with these rebellious people."

"Whatever intimidating look they throw your way, you will be able to look straight in their eyes the very same way."

"I will make you as stubborn, unyielding, and hard-headed as they are (but not in a sinful way)."

"I will give you absolute determination, which will be seen in your unstoppable resolve, purpose, fortitude, and grit."

Both God and difficult people can affect our countenances. Both God and others can control our smiles, our foreheads, our expressions, and our eyes. Both can . . . but only one will. The one we deem as the biggest, the most important, or the most relevant in our lives. So, what happens to you when the people in your life are big and the God in your life is small? How will those who intimidate you control the way you look? Take a look in the mirror and see who is controlling your appearance.

How do I learn to fear God as I should?

With each passage below, read what God says, think about it, and meditate on how His sovereignty personally affects you.

1 Samuel 12:24

Only fear the Lord, and serve him in truth with all your heart: for consider how great things he hath done for you.

Psalm 34:11–17

Come, ye children, hearken unto me: I will teach you the fear of the Lord. What man is he that desireth life, and loveth many days, that he may see good? Keep thy tongue from evil, and thy lips from speaking guile. Depart from evil, and do good; seek peace, and pursue it. The eyes of the Lord are upon the righteous, and his ears are open unto their cry. The face of the Lord is against them that do evil, to cut off the remembrance of them from the earth. The righteous cry, and the Lord heareth, and delivereth them out of all their troubles.

Proverbs 2:1–5

My son, if thou wilt receive my words, and hide my commandments with thee; so that thou incline thine ear unto wisdom, and apply thine heart to understanding; yea, if thou criest after knowledge, and liftest up thy voice for understanding; if thou seekest her as silver, and searchest for her as for hid treasures; then shalt thou understand the fear of the Lord, and find the knowledge of God.

FEAR 8

■ ■ ■

THE FEAR OF PUBLIC SPEAKING VS. THE FACT OF GOD'S GRACE

(THE FEAR OF EMBARRASSMENT, WITNESSING, SPEAKING IN PUBLIC, BEING RIDICULED, BEING MADE FUN OF, BEING DIFFERENT, ETC.)

This is what God says.

Jeremiah 1:6–8

Then said I, Ah, Lord God! behold, I cannot speak: for I am a child. But the Lord said unto me, Say not, I am a child: for thou shalt go to all that I shall send thee, and whatsoever I command thee thou shalt speak. Be not afraid of their faces: for I am with thee to deliver thee, saith the Lord.

Now think about it.

Jeremiah said, "Oh, my sovereign Lord and my almighty God! I cannot speak. I don't know how to speak. I do not have the maturity. I am nothing more than a little child and much too young to do this." But the Lord said to me, "Do not say, 'I am a youth,' because you will go everywhere I send you and you will speak everything I have commanded you to speak. Do not fear those you are speaking to; I will be with you. Do not be afraid of the way they look at you or show their disagreement on their faces, for I am with you to deliver you," says the Lord.

How can this affect me?

Among the top ten fears in life is the fear of public speaking. Some acquire this fear early in life when classmates laughed at their first oral report delivered in the third grade. Others were embarrassed in junior high school when they were called on to read in class with their constantly changing voices squeaking and squawking their way through the history report. The fear of standing before a crowd of peers and forgetting your lines is unbearable. Some would rather die. Knowing that everyone is staring at you wondering why anyone as stupid as you was chosen to speak in the first place is what nightmares are made of. Although this morbid

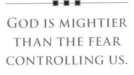

GOD IS MIGHTIER THAN THE FEAR CONTROLLING US.

fear of speaking in public keeps many from pursuing a career in politics, teaching, or preaching, it sadly keeps many from pursuing souls for Christ. The fear of witnessing paralyzes many Christians. The fear of sharing their faith with a resistant unbeliever keeps many in disobedience to the great commission. Jeremiah knew this fear. He was quick to find a seemingly good excuse for why he should not speak out for God. What excuses do you use? Jeremiah was asked by God to share God's truth with hardened, impetuous, disagreeable unbelievers. God has asked you to do the same. Jeremiah was asked by God to warn unbelievers of the consequences of their rejection of God's commands in His Word. God has asked you to do the same. Jeremiah was told by God to speak boldly against unrighteousness. God has asked you to do the same. Fear comes when we concentrate on the reception of the message and focus on those who may reject it. Confidence destroys fear when we concentrate on the message and focus on the One Who gave us the truth . . . God. Instead of focusing on your rejection, focus on the consequences of those who reject the truth of the gospel (eternal separation from God is a dreadful consequence). Instead of concentrating on what your listeners think about you, concentrate on what they think about God. God promised Jeremiah that He would be with him and deliver him. God promises us the same. God's omnipresence should be a comfort to our hearts each time we attempt to share the gospel. Deliverance indicates that the deliverer can overcome the power of the one previously in control. God's promise of deliverance presupposes that He is mightier than the fear that is controlling us. "Be not afraid! I am with you," says the Lord.

This is what God says.

Psalm 34:4
I sought the Lord, and he heard me, and delivered me from all my fears.

Now think about it.

I sought the Lord by diligently and carefully seeking to understand His will and His purpose for the matter that was causing me such debilitating fear. The all-knowing, ever-caring, almighty Jehovah God heard and answered me. He rescued me from the controlling hand of fear. He liberated me by overpowering the evil tyrant of anxiety. He delivered me from not just one or two of my fears, from not just the worries that trouble me the most, but from all my fears.

How can this affect me?

If I do not seek, I will not find. My deliverance is often conditional upon my seeking. If I refuse to seek God's will or purpose in a matter, God is under no obligation to deliver me. If my time is spent pampering my own concerns without attempting to see God's side of the issue, I may never experience God's deliverance. If I do not seek, I will not find. Why do I doubt God's deliverance? Why do I doubt that God will give me what is best for me? Do I really think that God wants to hurt me? Punish me? Destroy me? Do I expect Him to throw stones at me? Do I believe that He would send snakes into my life just to scare me? Do I forget what Jesus taught the multitudes on the mountainside (folks that faced testing and trials far greater than what most of us are presently facing)?

Ask, and it shall be given you; seek, and ye shall find; knock, and it shall be opened unto you: for every one that asketh receiveth; and he that seeketh findeth; and to him that knocketh it shall be opened. Or what man is there of you, whom if his son ask bread, will he give him a stone? Or if he ask a fish, will he give him a serpent? If ye then, being evil, know how to give good gifts unto your children, how much more shall your Father which is in heaven give good things to them that ask him? (Matthew 7:7–11)

If I want to be delivered from my fears, I must be willing to diligently seek God through His Word. If I want freedom from my fears, I must learn to pray for God's wisdom. Through such asking, I will determine that my fears are not based on His sovereignty but on my selfishness.

How do I know that God's grace is sufficient?

With each passage below, read what God says, think about it, and meditate on how His sovereignty personally affects you.

Ephesians 2:4–9

But God, who is rich in mercy, for his great love wherewith he loved us, even when we were dead in sins, hath quickened us together with Christ, (by grace ye are saved;) and hath raised us up together, and made us sit together in heavenly places in Christ Jesus: that in the ages to come he might shew the exceeding riches of his grace in his kindness toward us through Christ Jesus. For by grace are ye saved through faith; and that not of yourselves: it is the gift of God: not of works, lest any man should boast.

2 Corinthians 9:8

And God is able to make all grace abound toward you; that ye, always having all sufficiency in all things, may abound to every good work.

2 Corinthians 12:7–10

And lest I should be exalted above measure through the abundance of the revelations, there was given to me a thorn in the flesh, the messenger of Satan to buffet me, lest I should be exalted above measure. For this thing I besought the Lord thrice, that it might depart from me. And he said unto me, My grace is sufficient for thee: for my strength is made perfect in weakness. Most gladly therefore will I rather glory in my infirmities, that the power of Christ may rest upon me. Therefore I take pleasure in infirmities, in reproaches, in necessities, in persecutions, in distresses for Christ's sake: for when I am weak, then am I strong.

FEAR 9

■ ■ ■

THE FEAR OF RELATIONSHIPS VS. THE FACT OF GOD'S LOVE

(THE FEAR OF LIVING SINGLE, GETTING DIVORCED, NEVER BEING LOVED, NEVER BEING MARRIED, OR WONDERING IF EVEN GOD LOVES ME, ETC.)

This is what God says.

Luke 10:38-42

Now it came to pass, as they went, that he entered into a certain village: and a certain woman named Martha received him into her house. And she had a sister called Mary, which also sat at Jesus' feet, and heard his word. But Martha was cumbered about much serving, and came to him, and said, Lord, dost thou not care that my sister hath left me to serve alone? bid her therefore that she help me. And Jesus answered and said unto her, Martha, Martha, thou art careful and troubled about many things:

143

but one thing is needful: and Mary hath chosen that good part, which shall not be taken away from her.

Now think about it.

As they were traveling, Jesus entered into the small village of Bethany and a woman named Martha welcomed Him into her house. Martha had a sister, Mary, who sat at Jesus' feet listening to His teaching (while Martha was getting the meal ready). But Martha was consumed and felt as though she was being pulled in every direction (cumbered about) with all that had to be done to serve the meal. Martha came to Jesus and said, "Lord, do You not care that my sister, Mary (who is just sitting here listening to every word You say), has left me to serve and do all the work by myself? Tell her to help

IN OUR BUSYNESS WE FORGET CHRIST.

me!" Jesus kindly answered her, "Martha, Martha, you are anxious, worried, and troubled about the many things that you have to do (the work will get done and I am sure we will eat in time). Really, Martha, only one thing is truly necessary (that is getting to know Me through My words), and Mary has chosen that good thing, and what she learns from Me will not be taken away from her."

How can this affect me?

Martha was "stressed out!" Martha was "cumbered about." She was worried that she would not be accepted as a good hostess. She was afraid that everything would not be picture perfect. She was frazzled as she worked to serve an elaborate meal that really was not needed. She was working herself to the bone "serving" Christ when obviously she did not stop long enough to ask Him what He really wanted her to do. Many children grow up striving for acceptance and love by being good and performing properly only to be disappointed and discouraged by parents who are too busy or too selfish to care. All they want is to hear a few words of thanks or a quick hug of recognition. Those same children spend their adult lives "seeking" God's approval by "doing" and "serving," feverishly hoping to hear the words "Well done, My good and faithful servant."

The problem is that in our busyness we forget the "most needful thing," which is to know Christ. Martha served well but did not know Christ well. She actually questioned His love and care. "Lord, don't You care that I am left to do all the work by myself?" If you want to embarrass a Christian worker who has "burned out" of the ministry, simply ask him about his personal devotional life. We need Martha's hands and Mary's heart. Warren Wiersbe said, "It seems evident that the Lord wants each of us to imitate Mary in our worship and Martha in our work. Blessed are the balanced!" (*The Bible Exposition Commentary* [Colorado Springs: Chariot Victor Publishing, 1989.])

We live in an either/or rather than a both/and world. We often read a passage like this and attempt to choose which woman we are the most like and then get stressed out because we do not do enough or know enough. Your private time with God will give you all the assurance of His acceptance and the awareness of His love that you will need to serve Him throughout your day. Wouldn't it relieve the stress if you served God because you wanted to rather than because you had to? Sitting at His feet each morning will motivate you to serve by His side each day.

This is what God says.

1 John 4:16-18

And we have known and believed the love that God hath to us. God is love; and he that dwelleth in love dwelleth in God, and God in him. Herein is our love made perfect, that we may have boldness in the day of judgment: because as he is, so are we in this world. There is no fear in love; but perfect love casteth out fear: because fear hath torment. He that feareth is not made perfect in love.

Now think about it.

We have come to know, believe, and trust in the love God continually demonstrates to us. God is love and whoever lives and abides in love lives and abides in God and God lives and abides in him. By this one simple truth is our love matured and brought to perfection: as God is, so are we in this world. In other words, because God has so changed our selfish hearts that we now live with the same loving attitude that Jesus Christ lived with on earth, we can stand before God in judgment with the confidence that we will be accepted just like God accepted His Son, Jesus Christ, when He ascended to His Father after His resurrection. Our love has matured to the point that we will not be consumed with fear but hope to have boldness when we stand before God in the day of judgment. There is no fear in love; but perfect love casts out and does away with all fear because fear is consumed with the possibility of tormenting punishment. If you fear, you have not grown or matured in God's love.

How can this affect me?

We torment ourselves when we think about what might happen. The anticipation of a dentist's visit can be riddled with fear. A call to the principle's office can result in a long and fearful walk down the hall. When your boss sends a message that he needs to see you at the end of the day, the rest of the day can be spent in fear of what he is going to say. If we had to face God without any of our sins confessed and forgiven, we would and should dread that day of judgment. For the mature believer who realizes that because of God's love there is no condemnation to those of us who are in Christ Jesus, there is no penalty of sin to be paid because it has already been paid through the death of Jesus Christ, and there is no reconciliation to be addressed because we have been reconciled to Christ through His death, he can live without fear of the future. For the mature believer who realizes that because of God's love He has separated our sins from us as far as the east is from the west, He has hidden our sins behind His back and will choose to never bring them to His mind again, He has promised to judicially treat us just as if we had never sinned, he can joyfully look forward to standing in the presence of God. If we immaturely question God's love and forgiveness, we will tremble in fear as we approach His presence. (There certainly are many who cannot seem to get over certain sins of the past. They have gone to the Lord for forgiveness not once, but a thousand times. Their past sin controls their minds. Their guilt paralyzes their walk with God. It is at this time that we must think forgiven and act forgiven. This can be done through thanksgiving. Every time that ugly, old sin of the past comes to mind, instead of allowing guilt to take control, give gratitude the controls. Instead of asking for forgiveness again, thank God for the forgiveness He has already given. Instead of concentrating on how dirty you feel, concentrate on the fact that you were dirty but now are cleansed by the only One Who can cleanse and forgive . . . God.) If we truly believe what God promises us, if we are confident that His love has erased all our sin, if we trust His Word in what it promises about forgiveness, we will not fear. Perfect love equals no fear.

This is what God says.

James 2:19

Thou believest that there is one God; thou doest well: the devils also believe, and tremble.

Now think about it.

You believe that there is one God. Good! You're doing fine. But remember, even the demons (the evil spirits subject to Satan) believe that—and when they think of God (Who He is and what He can and will do), they tremble and shudder with extreme fear.

How can this affect me?

Why would anyone be afraid of a loving God? Why would anyone be so afraid of God that they tremble and shake in fear? Why would anyone be so scared of God that every hair on his head would bristle and stand on end? Why would anyone be so horrified by God that he shudders at the thought of standing in His presence? Why?

Here's your answer... eternal judgment. Everlasting punishment. Painful separation from God and loved ones forever and ever. Anyone who refuses to seek God's forgiveness for his wickedness should fear. Anyone who thinks that he can earn God's favor because he's "not really that bad" and is basically a "good person" should be afraid to stand before God. The demons James referred to seemed to know their eternal judgment and trembled at the thought of it. The demons had no problem with their theology and knew that God was not only fair and forgiving, but just and wrathful. God clearly warns every man of the consequences of rejecting Christ's gift of salvation. Many choose their sin over God. God, through His Word, pleads with sinners to repent, believe, and receive Christ. Many proudly refuse to believe. Why would anyone be afraid of a loving God? Why would anyone tremble and shake in fear at the thought of standing in God's presence? Because they reject Him. There is no other reason.

How do I know that God loves me?

With each passage below, read what God says, think about it, and meditate on how His sovereignty personally affects you.

1 John 4:9-11

In this was manifested the love of God toward us, because that God sent his only begotten Son into the world, that we might live through him. Herein is love, not that we loved God, but that he loved us, and sent his Son to be the propitiation for our sins. Beloved, if God so loved us, we ought also to love one another.

Romans 5:5-8

And hope maketh not ashamed; because the love of God is shed abroad in our hearts by the Holy Ghost which is given unto us. For when we were yet without strength, in due time Christ died for the ungodly. For scarcely for a righteous man will one die: yet peradventure for a good man some would even dare to die. But God commendeth his love toward us, in that, while we were yet sinners, Christ died for us.

1 John 4:16-19

And we have known and believed the love that God hath to us. God is love; and he that dwelleth in love dwelleth in God, and God in him. Herein is our love made perfect, that we may have boldness in the day of judgment: because as he is, so are we in this world. There is no fear in love; but perfect love casteth out fear: because fear hath torment. He that feareth is not made perfect in love. We love him, because he first loved us.

FEAR **10**

■ ■ ■

THE FEAR OF WASTING MY LIFE VS. THE FACT OF GOD'S WILL

(THE FEAR OF JUDGMENT, MISSING GOD'S WILL, WASTING MY LIFE, LIVING A MEANINGLESS EXISTENCE, STANDING BEFORE GOD WITH NOTHING TO OFFER, ETC.)

This is what God says.

Exodus 20:20

And Moses said unto the people, Fear not: for God is come to prove you, and that his fear may be before your faces, that ye sin not.

Now think about it.

And Moses said unto the people as they trembled in fear at God's awesome presence, "Don't be afraid. God is come to test you and to prove to you that His way is best for both your good and His glory. God will also show you that the fear, respect, and reverence you show toward Him (the fearful respect that is so constantly on your mind) will keep you from sinning.

How can this affect me?

Most of us are controlled by either good fear or bad fear. God commands us to fear in one verse and commands us not to fear in another. God encourages the right kind of fear and discourages the wrong kind of fear. Learning the difference between the two kinds of fear makes all the difference in the way we fear. The people of Israel stood frightened at the smoke, lightning, and fire on Mount Sinai as God met with Moses, giving him the divine laws that were designed to protect the identity of God's people forever. Israel, knowing their own selfish hearts and the many times they had doubted God, mistrusted God, and even spoke against God, shuddered at the thought of being in His presence. In all reality, we should shudder too. Are you any different from the Israelites in the way you have treated your Lord?

> **WHAT IF GOD GAVE YOU WHAT YOU TRULY DESERVE?**

Can you imagine what that day will be like when you personally kneel before God? He knows your selfish heart. He could list every time you have doubted Him. He could read aloud for all to hear the times you thought He was unfair or didn't care. There will be no opportunity for denial, excuses, or blame shifting. He is God! All-knowing! Omniscient! He not only knows all, He has the power, the authority, even the right to give us the fair and just consequences for our selfishness, doubt, disrespect, and sin. What if God gave you what you truly deserve? His mercy that keeps us from hell; His forgiveness that separates our sin from us as far as the east is from the west; His grace that cleanses us from all unrighteousness should cause us to be overwhelmed with humble thankfulness. Knowing the depravity of our own hearts, it will be hard to look our Lord in the eyes. I doubt very much that any of us will walk up to God and give Him a big high-five! We will do what Moses' people did; we will tremble in fear. And we should! He is an awesome, awe-inspiring God. There is good fear and bad fear. Which controls you?

This is what God says.

Proverbs 3:21–26

My son, let not them depart from thine eyes: keep sound wisdom and discretion: so shall they be life unto thy soul, and grace to thy neck. Then shalt thou walk in thy way safely, and thy foot shall not stumble. When thou liest down, thou shalt not be afraid: yea, thou shalt lie down, and thy sleep shall be sweet. Be not afraid of sudden fear, neither of the desolation of the wicked, when it cometh. For the Lord shall be thy confidence, and shall keep thy foot from being taken.

Now think about it.

My son, guard, protect, and keep sound wisdom and discretion and don't let either one of them vanish from your sight. Such wisdom and discretion will give you an inner joy of living (life to your soul) and a graciousness of spirit and attitude (adornment or grace to your neck). Each step you take in life will be based on godly wisdom, which results in the security of knowing that you are exactly where God wants you to be. Each path you choose to follow will be chosen through biblical discretion, and you will not spend your life stumbling and falling on time-consuming and thought-controlling rabbit trails.

When you lie down to go to sleep each night, you will not be afraid of what will happen through the night or even the next day. When you go to bed, your sleep will be sweet (you will sleep soundly), and you will not spend hours in bed tossing and turning, trying to force the fearful pressures of life out of your mind. Do not lay in bed at night fearfully thinking of sudden, unexpected disasters that could happen to you or your family. Do not fear the devastation and the ruin that the wicked will someday experience. Remember, the Lord will be your confidence. The Lord will keep your foot from being snared, caught, or trapped. The Lord will keep you and protect you through sound wisdom and discretion.

How can this affect me?

Over-the-counter sleep aids are a hot item. Sound sleep evades the fearful. The tossing and turning of the soul seems to cause the same in sleep. A lack of confidence in God results in a lack of rest at night. If you crave a good night's sleep, you must secure the wisdom and discretion that comes from God Himself. God promises to give wisdom to those who ask for it (James 1:5). Wisdom, in a way, is seeing through the eyes of

God. Discretion relies on wisdom to make good judgments and wise choices in everyday life. Knowing that the decision you made was a wise, godly decision can help you sleep with confidence. Wise discretion protects you from tripping and falling. Each day that you walk through life without falling into sin helps you to rest in God's goodness at night. Your sleep will be sweet when guilt is nonexistent. Your sleep will be sweet when you do not have to fear that someone will find out what you have done. Your sleep will be sweet when you do not spend your night prayers begging God to forgive you for your wickedness. Your sleep will be sweet when by wisdom and discretion you have walked a day with God confidently saying no to temptation and yes to righteousness. Wise decisions and discreet judgments are much better than any sleep aid on the market today. Have a good night's sleep!

How do I know that God has a purpose for my life?

With each passage below, read what God says, think about it, and meditate on how His sovereignty personally affects you.

Romans 8:27–29

And he that searcheth the hearts knoweth what is the mind of the Spirit, because he maketh intercession for the saints according to the will of God. And we know that all things work together for good to them that love God, to them who are the called according to his purpose. For whom he did foreknow, he also did predestinate to be conformed to the image of his Son, that he might be the firstborn among many brethren.

1 Thessalonians 5:9–11

For God hath not appointed us to wrath, but to obtain salvation by our Lord Jesus Christ, who died for us, that, whether we wake or sleep, we should live together with him. Wherefore comfort yourselves together, and edify one another, even as also ye do.

Ephesians 5:1–2

Be ye therefore followers of God, as dear children; and walk in love, as Christ also hath loved us, and hath given himself for us an offering and a sacrifice to God for a sweet smelling savor.

2 Timothy 1:7

For God hath not given us the spirit of fear; but of power, and of love, and of a sound mind.